Student Workbook

When Words Collide
A Media Writer's Guide to Grammar and Style

NINTH EDITION

Tracy Ilene Miller

Core book by

Lauren Kessler
University of Oregon

Duncan McDonald
University of Oregon

CENGAGE
Learning·

Australia • Brazil • Mexico • Singapore • United Kingdom • United States

ISBN: 978-1-305-41106-7

Cengage Learning
20 Channel Center Street
Boston, MA 02210
USA

Cengage Learning is a leading provider of customized learning solutions with office locations around the globe, including Singapore, the United Kingdom, Australia, Mexico, Brazil, and Japan. Locate your local office at:
www.cengage.com/global.

Cengage Learning products are represented in Canada by Nelson Education, Ltd.

To learn more about Cengage Learning Solutions, visit **www.cengage.com**.

Purchase any of our products at your local college store or at our preferred online store **www.cengagebrain.com**.

For product information and technology assistance, contact us at
Cengage Learning Customer & Sales Support, 1-800-354-9706.

For permission to use material from this text or product, submit all requests online at
www.cengage.com/permissions
Further permissions questions can be emailed to
permissionrequest@cengage.com.

Printed in the United States of America
Print Number: 01   Print Year: 2014

Contents

Contents

PREFACE

In this ninth edition of the workbook for *When Words Collide,* an aspect of communications that has greatly expanded in our world since the last edition — social media — gets a nod for its impact on the way we obtain information. In one of the exercises in this new edition, I challenge you to find the errors in several social media posts as if you were an editor reviewing the work. The exercise represents the kind of errors I see every day in my communications, marketing and public relations work.

It's true that social media relies on interactions more informal than other forms of communications. But it still relies on precise and grammatically correct constructions, especially for business-related social media sites. The number of digital feeds available to us may be growing, but the requirements of grammar proficiency — of correct writing — endure. Why? Because whether you oversee social media, write blogs and online news articles or participate in any other form of content creation for a mass audience, errors cause readers to pause and cause reader confusion.

Actually, it's hard to know which happens first, the pause or the confusion. But in either case, readers who focus on their confusion are readers whose attention is pulled from the content. If the eternal goal of a writer is to be understood, and perhaps for readers to be captured or enthralled by the content, then the job falls flat when reader attention is instead pulled toward errors. More often than not, you lose your readers, who move on and away from the writing. In the process, credibility can suffer.

When this exercise book was first conceived by Duncan McDonald (and thank you for that, Duncan) 30 years ago, it was designed to provide students of grammar a place to test their comprehension of the rules. Through each edition of the workbook, it has been expanded to be much more than that, and even more so in this most recent edition: to further pinpoint the kinds of errors that new writers and students new to English are *most likely to make* in constructing English sentences. It includes a kind of survey of errors that comes from my more than 20 years of reading student papers and editing client work.

So, in your quest to learn grammar and to complete the exercises in this book, pay close attention to your own progress and comprehension of the concepts. Understanding why you got an answer right or wrong will go a long way in helping you the next time you begin to edit your own work, and the time after that. Although the words are changing in your writing, the grammar rules remain the same. The trick is to practice good grammar enough times that you see the pattern of the rules in your writing, to make you your own best editor. My hope is that the breadth of exercises in this book provides you that solid footing, to repeat your application of the grammar rules to gain proficiency in them enough that you begin to apply them to your own writing. And then, you just keep practicing.

For instructors, the answers to the exercises are available at the following Web site:

<u>www.login.cengage.com</u>

For students, instructors will work with you to explain the answers, if needed, and to offer even more challenges as you strengthen your writing skills.

Learning grammar is a lifelong process. Through the exercises in this workbook, you'll be led through a journey of breaking down sentences into their parts, and then ensuring those parts are put back together — correctly.

Good luck.

Tracy Ilene Miller

EXERCISE 1 • TYPES OF SENTENCES

Purpose   To correctly identify sentence types.

Reference   "When Words Collide" (9/e), Chapter 3

Directions   Please use the following code to identify the sentence
                     types:
                     (A) simple (B) compound (C) complex
                     (D) compound-complex (E) fragment

no verb

____ 1.   According to my homeroom teacher, all students need to
           check in with her before sitting down.

____ 2.   Lifting all those sandbags and carrying them more than
           three blocks to the dangerously stressed levee.

____ 3.   The prosecutor wanted to introduce a piece of evidence,
           but the judge told her she would have to wait for the
           defense to review it.

____ 4.   Tamara, who visited Oregon this month, has a new
           perspective on living in the Northwest.

____ 5.   Piper cringed when her mom smoked in the kitchen.

____ 6.   I'm making a comprehensive list of all my favorite gourmet
           treats.

____ 7.   Working until the sun came over the top of the hill.

____ 8.   When Juan bought a new baseball glove, he would rub it
           with conditioner, put the ball in the glove, tie it with string
           and leave it in the sunlight to warm the leather, which
           made the glove easy to shape.

____ 9.   Help me; I'm trying to get the wrinkles out of this shirt.

____ 10.   Sharon and Bartok were expected to not only place but to
           win the watermelon-eating contest.

____ 11.   The white cat and the gigantic brown grizzly bear made a
           strange pair of playmates, but they had been friends since
           they were newborns.

Exercise 1 ■ Types of Sentences

_____ 12. Sherman signed up for the last shift at work, and then went home to sleep.

_____ 13. He left the airport because it was too crowded.

_____ 14. Don't you think she is a fabulous actor?

_____ 15. Carly enjoys collecting seashells and pipe cleaners.

NAME _____   SCORE _____

EXERCISE 2 • THE BASIC SENTENCE: THE SUBJECT AND ITS VERB

Purpose   To correctly identify the subject of a sentence.

To correctly identify subjects as actors always paired with verbs.

To understand subject–verb combinations as the basic unit of all sentences.

Reference   "When Words Collide" (9/e), Chapters 3 and 4

Directions   Select the correct answer from the options provided, or fill in the blanks as directed.

____ 1.   Which noun, acting as the subject, is linked to the verb in this sentence?
At noon, the sound of the choir carried through the cathedral.
A.   noon
B.   sound
C.   choir
D.   cathedral

2.   What is the verb in sentence 1?

_____

_____

____ 3.   How many verbs are in this sentence?
I wanted to finish all my homework, but the sun burst out from behind the clouds, and the birds were singing to me, "Go play."
A.   two
B.   three
C.   four
D.   five

4.   List the verbs you identified in question 3.

_____

_____

____ 5. How many subjects are in this sentence?
When she read about kale popsicles, Lucille thought it
would be a great way to get her little Henry to eat his
vegetables.
A. one
B. two
C. three
D. four

____ 6. What are the subjects in this sentence?
The market steadied today after the government eased fears
by depositing billions in the Treasury to stabilize the
financial sector.
A. market, government
B. market, government, sector
C. government, Treasury, sector

7. Why is *Sophia, Kyle and Prita* considered the subject of this
sentence?
Sophia, Kyle and Prita coordinated the university blood drive again
this year.

_____

_____

____ 8. How many verbs are in the following sentence?
Unable to purchase an Egyptian visa, the traveler decided
to take a bus to Jordan instead.
A. one
B. two
C. three
D. four

9. In the following sentence, *to nourish* sounds like an action word.
Succinctly, and using grammar terms you already know, explain
why it is *not* a verb.
Fresh vegetable juices provide nutrients that are easily absorbed to
nourish growth of healthy cells.

_____

_____

10. Underline and identify all the subjects and verbs in the following
sentence.
I absolutely can do the tango wearing flip-flops, although I'd prefer
not to.

w-4

11. Underline and identify all the subjects and verbs in the following sentence.
    My mother said I should wear my clothes two days in a row before I put them in the laundry hamper.

12. In one clear sentence, using grammar terms you already know, tell how to recognize the subject of a sentence.

    _____

    _____

___ 13. How many verbs are in this sentence?
    The fifth grader told his classmates that, if they voted for him, he guaranteed donuts for lunch 10 times during the school year.
    A. one
    B. two
    C. three
    D. four

14. What is/are the subject(s) of the verbs in sentence 13?

    _____

    _____

15. In the following sentence, *completing* sounds like an action word. Succinctly, and using grammar terms you already know, explain why it is *not* a verb.
    After completing his first marathon, Zachary suddenly collapsed.

    _____

    _____

16. Underline and identify all the subjects and verbs in the following sentence.
    Ahmad's recently published research on the flow of sediment in streams was widely accepted by his peers.

___ 17. How many subjects are in the following sentence?
    After the student driver grabbed the steering wheel, she closed her eyes and slammed her foot on the brake to prevent her front wheels from falling into the ditch.
    A. one
    B. two
    C. three
    D. four

18. List the subjects in sentence 17.

_____

_____

19. List the verbs in sentence 17.

_____

_____

20. What is the subject of this sentence?
    Please wait your turn.

_____

_____

NAME _____   SCORE _____

EXERCISE 3 • FIND THE VERB!

Purpose   To develop mastery of verb conjugation.

To recognize auxiliary verbs as part of verb strings with main verbs.

To recognize verbs, even when they are separated from their subjects.

Reference   "When Words Collide" (9/e), Chapters 3, 4 and 8

____ 1.   What is the complete verb in the following sentence?
The fires have been smoldering all night in the northern part of the state.
    A. have been smoldering
    B. have
    C. smoldering
    D. have been

2.   What is/are the verb(s) in the following sentence?
The doctors insisted that treating the tumor with chemotherapy was the only viable solution.

_____

_____

3.   What is/are the verb(s) in the following sentence?
The bicyclist was speeding down the mountain and, to everyone's surprise, passed the car the last quarter mile before reaching town.

_____

_____

____ 4.   What constitutes the verb(s) in this sentence?
The candidate has been steadily campaigning for two years, and the electorate is expected to vote him into office next week.
    A. has been steadily campaigning, is expected
    B. campaigning, is expected, to vote
    C. has been campaigning, is expected
    D. has been, is

5. What is the complete verb in this sentence?
Will anything persuade Jill not to take a kayak over Niagara Falls?

_____

_____

6. What is/are the verb(s) in the following sentence?
With the new ruling, classes of at least 60 minutes are required in all elementary schools.

_____

_____

7. What is/are the verb(s) in the following sentence?
The company chose a new logo, in addition to a new color for its branding, and decided to present it at the next stockholders' meeting.

_____

_____

8–20 Directions

Complete the following sentences by supplying the proper conjugation of the infinitive form of the verb provided under each blank space.

Although he _____ his job as a beat reporter for the local
      8. *to enjoy* (present tense)

newspaper, he _____ always uncomfortable with the
      9. *to be* (present perfect)

wreckage he _____ of automobile accidents.
      10. *to see* (present tense)

Many seniors graduating from college _____ to move back in
               11. *to plan* (present tense)

with their parents.

The shop owner _____ the professional dog walker who

12. *to sue* (present progressive)

_____ providing services last month in the next door building

13. *to begin* (simple past)

over damages to his storefront by some of the dogs he _____

14. *to say* (present tense)

_____ out of control.

15. *to be* (present tense)

Six friends, whose relationship _____ back as far as

16. *to go* (present tense)

kindergarten, _____ the unique and lively music of the new

17. *to create* (present tense)

high school band, Go Back to School.

Antique violins _____ his passion, and he _____

18. *to be* (present tense)   19. *to take* (present perfect)

several trips to Italy to study the craft.

She shuns ice cream while training for marathons and instead

_____ lots of yogurt.

20. *to substitute* (present tense)

NAME _____   SCORE _____

EXERCISE 4 • PROPER USE OF VOICE

Purpose   To identify active and passive voice.

To identify the constructions that are better suited to passive voice.

To learn to write more forcefully and crisply by using active voice constructions.

Reference   "When Words Collide" (9/e), Chapters 3 and 8

1–5 Directions

Select the correct answer from the options provided, or fill in the answer as directed.

____ 1.   Which of the following choices places this sentence in active voice?
The sugar water _____ the hummingbirds.
A.   was relished by
B.   satiated

____ 2.   Which of the following choices places this sentence in passive voice?
The student body _____ the trees would be cut down.
A.   was not informed
B.   protested that

____ 3.   Which sentence construction do you think is the best choice, given the information?
A.   This weekend, as expected, the decrease in student studying was due to the warm, unseasonable weather.
B.   The decrease in student studying this weekend, because of the warm, unseasonable weather, was to be expected.
C.   Professors at the school said they had expected that students would study less during the unseasonably warm weekend weather.
D.   The warm, unseasonable weather, which was expected, caused students to study less.

4. What voice, active or passive, does the sentence use that you chose in question 3?

_____

_____

5. Why did you choose the sentence you did in question 3?

_____

_____

6–18 Directions

Active voice makes the subject of the sentence perform. In most writing, the subject acts rather than is acted upon. In the following passive voice sentences, underline the agent who (or that) performs the action. Then, unless passive voice is more effective, rewrite the sentence in the active voice. If you make no change to a sentence, explain your decision. If necessary, "tighten" any wordy constructions.

Example	After the wedding rehearsal, there was a four-course dinner served by <u>Robin Bullock</u>.
Rewrite	Robin Bullock served a four-course dinner after the wedding rehearsal.

(The actor or agent *[Robin Bullock]* now is more prominent in the sentence, and the action is more direct.)

6. The baseball was drilled by Gareth past the stunned batter on the first pitch.

_____

_____

7. The report on poverty by the nonprofit organization was quickly compiled and was submitted to the governor.

_____

_____

8. At dawn, the pitiful moaning of a wildebeest, which was wounded, was heard.

_____

_____

9. The meeting was gaveled to order by Paula Miles, who was serving as interim president.

    _____

    _____

10. Several bags of rice were thrown by the guests of the wedding at the end of the ceremony.

    _____

    _____

11. Former governor Edward Edwards was arrested last night for speeding.

    _____

    _____

12. A defense appropriation measure to guarantee the funding of "drone" spy planes will be considered tomorrow by the House Armed Services Committee.

    _____

    _____

13. The negative effect on your class performance because of text-messaging every class period has been noticed by your professors.

    _____

    _____

14. The school superintendent was robbed by a thief wearing a ski mask.

    _____

    _____

15. The 200-pound marlin was wrestled to the deck by four burly fishermen.

    _____

    _____

16. We were asked by our new boss to count the staplers in the office before leaving for the day.

_____

_____

17. The proposed increase in fees will be bitterly opposed by the students.

_____

_____

18. There is a considerable range of skill demonstrated by the new graduates.

_____

_____

19. Read the following passage. Rewrite the ideas in active voice, eliminating wordiness and awkward constructions if necessary.

    The new federal nutrition regulations for schools were designed to help end the obesity epidemic in America, but just because school districts have to create regulations on the availability of junk food does not mean children will not have access to it.

_____

_____

_____

20. Rewrite the following sentence to be more direct and less wordy.

    At the community meeting with the legislator, there was a heated argument between two of the community members attending that legislators should enforce stricter dangerous dog codes, such as breed-specific bans or a zero tolerance bite policy, to reduce the amount of preventable dog attacks.

_____

_____

_____

Based on your rewrite, your readings, and any class discussion on defensible uses of passive voice, explain your decision to use either active or passive voice. Why is the one you chose better than the other?

_____

_____

_____

EXERCISE 5 • VERB TYPES

Purpose   To correctly identify the verb forms.

                     To show the relationship of verb parts to other parts
                     of the sentence.

Reference   "When Words Collide" (9/e), Chapter 4

Directions   Underline the verb or verbs in each sentence. It's
                     possible that there will be more than one verb type in
                     the sentence. In the space provided at the left,
                     indicate whether the verb is transitive (T), intransitive
                     (I), or linking (L). If the verb is transitive, circle its
                     direct object. If the verb is linking, circle its predicate
                     nominative or predicate adjective. **Note:** If a
                     numbered item does not contain a verb, mark SF
                     (sentence fragment) in the space.

Example   Snow and high winds <u>closed</u> the (Denver airport) this
                     morning.
                     (T—Verb is transitive. It has a direct object, *Denver*
                     airport.)

____ 1.   Sacramento is the capital of California.

____ 2.   Thank goodness the rain has stopped!

____ 3.   The appeals court upheld the lower court decision.

____ 4.   Driven by violent winds, the storm struck the coast with
            great fury.

____ 5.   I constantly dream of great fame and fortune.

____ 6.   Dreaming of chocolate all day long.

____ 7.   Tripping over the sleeping dog, he fell down and lost
            consciousness.

____ 8.   Swimming, running and cycling are parts of a demanding
            triathlon.

___ 9.   To win this prestigious race, an important goal for him.

___ 10.   Emily Anderson, who won the Des Moines Marathon, will run the Charlotte Marathon on April 29.

___ 11.   You'll never guess whom Tito is dating!

___ 12.   Do you know how to build a den for a platypus?

___ 13.   Please stop!

___ 14.   You are on the grounds of the University of Oregon, heralded as one of the most beautiful campuses in the United States.

___ 15.   She is researching the impact of "blog" journalism.

___ 16.   Wait!

___ 17.   Because of rapidly declining profits, the board decided to fire its chief executive officer.

___ 18.   Icy conditions sent drivers skidding off the highway.

___ 19.   Arun seems quite friendly, don't you think?

___ 20.   The newly appointed commissioner appears concerned about her new role.

21–25 Directions

Provide the appropriate verb type and tense as indicated in the parentheses.

21.   The city's budget _____ doomed, according to
                        (linking verb, present tense)
      press reports.

22.   A new vote on the budget _____ soon, the councilors
                            (intransitive verb, future tense)
      hope.

23.   Her agent _____ the station's offer of contract
               (transitive verb, past tense)
      renewal.

24. _____!
    (intransitive verb, present tense)

25. Voters _____ the parking resolution but
    (transitive verb, present tense)

    _____ the public safety budget.

    (transitive verb, present tense)

EXERCISE 6 • SINGULARS AND PLURALS

Purpose   To develop mastery of verb conjugation.

To recognize singular subjects and plural subjects.

To know that *s* at the end of a verb does not denote plural conjugation of the verb.

Reference   "When Words Collide" (9/e), Chapters 4 and 6

1–5 Directions

Choose the correct conjugation of the verb from the answers provided.

___ 1.   The housesitter _____ the mail for all the roommates when they are on vacation.
A. collect
B. collects
C. collecting

___ 2.   His new dog, Luca, and the older puppy, Bonnie, _____ fetch together.
A. plays
B. play
C. plays'
D. playing

___ 3.   Many experts _____ some of the negative campaigning _____ run its course.
A. believes, has
B. believe, have
C. believes, have
D. believe, has

___ 4.   The justices in the case _____ the ruling will go into effect at the end of the year.
A. says
B. say
C. saying

____ 5.   Carly's interest in ballet, music and art _____ she is a focused child.
A. proves
B. prove
C. proving

6–10 Directions

Complete the following sentences by supplying the proper conjugation of the infinitive form of the verb provided under each blank space.

6. Shelby, Spider and Lee _____ several shows a week in the
                to play (present tense)
San Francisco area.

7. Surveys and interviews of the people who went on the cruise more than once _____ a preference for lavish meals over expensive
           to reveal (present tense)
entertainment.

8. Those two large farms by the foothills of the mountain outside of town _____ owned by the same landholder.
      to be (present perfect)

9. The book, translated into three languages and made into several movies, _____ scheduled for a worldwide release after
        to be (present perfect)
this year's Academy Awards ceremony.

10. A glut of movies using computer animation _____
                        to have (present perfect)
cooled audience interest in the once-novel format.

11–15 Directions

In each of the following sentences there is a verb conjugation error. Circle the incorrect verb form and write the correct one on the line provided underneath the sentence. **Note:** There is only one conjugation error and there are no other errors to find in the sentence.

11. The writing in the second-year students' portfolios were surprisingly advanced.

_____

_____

12. There is many ways to learn how to drive, but he was unsure of which one to choose.

    _____

    _____

13. Measles are one of the diseases pediatricians warn parents about most.

    _____

    _____

14. To the annoyance of her friends, she often give away the plot of new movies in her blog posts.

    _____

    _____

15. The benefits of daily exercise and healthful eating is often ignored until we reach middle age.

    _____

    _____

NAME _____   SCORE _____

EXERCISE 7 • VERBALS: THEY'RE NOT IN THE DRIVER'S SEAT!

Purpose   To correctly identify all verbal types and to
                         distinguish them from verbs.

Reference   "When Words Collide" (9/e), Chapter 4

1–5 Directions

Choose the correct response from the choices offered.

____ 1.   Which one of the following parts of speech cannot be a
            verbal?
            A.   noun
            B.   adverb
            C.   adjective
            D.   preposition

____ 2.   Which one of the following verbals cannot be the subject of
            a sentence?
            A.   gerund
            B.   participle
            C.   infinitive
            D.   A verbal cannot act as the subject of a sentence.

____ 3.   Which verbal is always a noun?
            A.   participle
            B.   gerund
            C.   infinitive

____ 4.   Which of the following three sentences does not contain a
            verbal?
            A.   All of the campers who attended the workshop knew
                 how to pitch a tent.
            B.   The party couldn't start without the arrival of the hired
                 clown.
            C.   I forgot to tell her that running in the park after dark
                 can be dangerous.

_____ 5.   What is the only verb in the following sentence?
A severe rainstorm lashed the South Carolina coast last night, followed today by the heaviest snowfall to hit that state in the last 30 years.
     A.   lashed
     B.   followed
     C.   heaviest
     D.   hit

Bonus Question

How many verbals are in sentence 5? What are they?

_____

6–15 Directions

Each of the following 10 sentences contains one verbal phrase. Indicate the correct verbal using this code:
     G   Gerund phrase
     P   Participial phrase
     I   Infinitive phrase

_____ 6.   He finished his class project in three days, barely pausing to eat or sleep.

_____ 7.   The former CEO volunteered to work with Habitat for Humanity.

_____ 8.   Is it really that difficult to identify a verbal?

_____ 9.   Homer really enjoys eating corn dogs.

_____ 10.   The judges seated at the table were laughing and joking.

_____ 11.   Buffeted by gale-force winds, he could barely walk across the street.

_____ 12.   Jack could not persuade his mother to take the magic beans.

_____ 13.   I appreciate your sending a care package to me with some dark chocolate caramels.

_____ 14.   You are on the grounds of the University of Oregon, long heralded as one of the most beautiful campuses in the United States.

____ 15.   He knew enough to bring an umbrella to all the home games.

Bonus Question

Write one sentence that contains all three verbal forms. Just one sentence—you can do this!

_____

_____

_____

16–20 Directions

This final section deals with subject–verb agreement and proper use of modifiers involving verbals. Choose the correct answer from the choices offered.

Example   Restoring old houses (A. is B. are) both her hobby and her business.

Answer: A. is. The subject of this sentence is the gerund *Restoring.* Gerunds always take a singular verb. The gerund's object, *houses,* does not control the number of the verb.

____ 16.   What is the participial phrase in the following sentence? Returning from his six-week trip, Paul promised never to embark on such an incredibly grueling backpacking adventure ever again.
A.   promised
B.   incredibly grueling
C.   never to embark
D.   Returning from his six-week trip

____ 17.   And what does that participial phrase modify in sentence 16?
A.   trip
B.   Paul
C.   adventure
D.   promised

____ 18.   Sending short notes to her friends (A. has B. have) helped Sara combat homesickness.

w-27

____ 19. What does the participial phrase in the following sentence modify?
Working around the clock, his project was finished three hours before the deadline.
A. hours
B. deadline
C. clock
D. project
E. Actually, the phrase "dangles" and is incorrectly written. It doesn't logically modify the subject of the main clause.

____ 20. Yelling outside at the top of her lungs (A. feel B. feels) good after studying in the library for eight hours straight.

EXERCISE 8 • A GERUND IS NOT A PARTICIPLE — AND VICE VERSA!

Purpose   To correctly identify *–ed* and *–ing* words according to their part of speech in increasingly complicated sentences.

To distinguish gerunds from participles.

Reference   "When Words Collide" (9/e), Chapters 5 and 6

1–6 Directions

Choose the correct response from the choices offered. When asked to rewrite sentences, use the space provided to do so.

___ 1.   In this sentence, what kind of verbal is contained in the underlined phrase?
Gail was named the game MVP <u>for catching the most fly balls</u>.
A.   infinitive
B.   gerund
C.   participle
D.   adverbial

___ 2.   What part of speech is the verbal in the sentence above?
A.   noun
B.   pronoun
C.   adverb
D.   adjective

___ 3.   Why is the underlined word in the following sentence *not* a participle?
Jasmine was <u>bored</u> with waiting for her mother to drive her to school.
A.   It is part of an infinitive phrase.
B.   It is a predicate nominative.
C.   It is part of the transitive verb.
D.   It is part of the intransitive verb.

____ 4.   What is the role of the underlined word in this sentence? The runners <u>jogging</u> down the wooded path did not see the lion waiting in the grass.

    A. With *did not see*, it is the second action word, or verb, of the sentence.

    B. It is an adjective that provides a description of the runners.

    C. It is the noun subject of the clause that begins *jogging down the wooded path*.

    D. It is the beginning of a participial phrase.

    E. It is both B and D.

____ 5.   What's the error in this sentence? After throwing a 96-mph curve ball, the batter was struck out by the pitcher.

    A. dangling modifier

    B. word usage

    C. passive voice

    D. both A and C

6.   In the space provided, rewrite the sentence in item 5 to correct the error(s).

_____

_____

7–10 Directions

Each of these sentences has three *–ing* words. In the space provided, write the part of speech of the word and its function in the sentence.

Example   After traveling to a remote corner of the Oregon desert, the hiking team attached a huge tarp to the rocks, creating a large enclosure that protected them from the elements.

traveling: noun; object of the prepositional phrase beginning with *after*

hiking: adjective; a modifier of the noun *team*

creating: adjective; begins the participial phrase that ends with *enclosure*

7. A rendering of the new student union, with its soaring five-story wall and curved ceiling, is framed on his wall.

    rendering: _____

    soaring: _____

    ceiling: _____

8. As a way of hiding her disdain for compromise, Yuki often goes searching for blame in others, effectively alienating them.

    hiding: _____

    searching: _____

    alienating: _____

9. Avoiding her friends who lived by the marina was Jessica's way of dealing with her fear of deep-sea diving.

    avoiding: _____

    dealing: _____

    diving: _____

10. Shuji decided that drinking green tea and taking vitamins were two strategies for preventing too many colds.

    drinking: _____

    taking: _____

    preventing: _____

11–13 Directions

In each of the following sentences, there are three *–ed* words. In the space provided, write the part of speech of the word and, briefly, the purpose of the word as a function of its part of speech.

11. The manager's convoluted instructions frustrated his employees, creating palpable tensions in the meetings between him and already overworked workers.

    convoluted: _____

    frustrated: _____

    overworked: _____

12. He decided to leave the movie because the theater was too crowded and the heat system continuously blasted hot air into the room.

    decided: _____

    crowded: _____

    blasted: _____

13. Don't accept that widely circulated and expanded story about the embezzlement unless you have adequately researched it.

    circulated: _____

    expanded: _____

    researched: _____

14–15 Directions

Choose the correct response from the choices offered.

____ 14. Which of the following sentences contains a dangling modifier?
   A. She's a great athlete, rarely tiring during an event.
   B. Discovering a zero balance in my bank account, a credit card was needed to complete the transaction.
   C. Although he studied for more than a week and literally copied parts of two texts.
   D. Remember everything the professor demanded.

____ 15. What is the proper term for the underlined section in the sentence that follows?
   Ruby enjoys <u>reading about women scientists</u> of the early 20th century.
   A. gerund phrase
   B. participial phrase
   C. direct object
   D. A and C
   E. None of the above

NAME _____   SCORE _____

EXERCISE 9 • NOUNS AND PRONOUNS AS SUBJECTS AND OBJECTS

Purpose   To connect understanding of nouns and pronouns
                     with sentence elements.

Reference   "When Words Collide" (9/e), Chapters 4 and 6

Directions   Indicate the letter of the correct answer.

___ 1.   How many pronouns are in the following sentence?
            Who went to the commissary and forgot to get me some
            candy?
            A.   one
            B.   two
            C.   three
            D.   four

___ 2.   How many subjects are in the following sentence?
            My teachers think that studying Latin in school is a waste
            of time.
            A.   none
            B.   one
            C.   two
            D.   three

___ 3.   List those subjects.

_____

4.   Of all the subjects in sentence 2, how many are pronouns?
            A.   none
            B.   one
            C.   two
            D.   three

___ 5.   List those pronouns, if any.

_____

_____ 6. What is the direct object in the following sentence?
Billy gave Tommy a dirty look after the presentation.
A. Billy
B. Tommy
C. look
D. presentation

7. Sentence 6 contains two other grammatical "objects." List them
below according to their grammatical terms.

Indirect object _____

Object of preposition _____

_____ 8. <u>Rita Mae Brown</u> is classified as what part of speech?
A. common noun
B. proper noun
C. personal pronoun
D. relative pronoun

_____ 9. What is the subject of the following sentence?
Unable to purchase an Egyptian visa, the traveler decided
to take a bus to Jordan instead.
A. visa
B. traveler
C. bus

_____ 10. How many nouns are in the following sentence?
The market steadied today after the Treasury stabilized the
financial sector.
A. none
B. one
C. two
D. three

_____ 11. How many subject(s) is/are in the following sentence?
Running in the rain is great if you have waterproof shoes.
A. none
B. one
C. two
D. three

_____ 12. List the subjects.

_____

____ 13.   What is the possessive form of the personal pronoun *she?*
    A.   she's
    B.   her's
    C.   their
    D.   her

____ 14.   Why is *homicides* in the following sentence not its subject?
The rate of homicides in the county is dropping rapidly.
    A.   It is the direct object.
    B.   It is the indirect object.
    C.   It is the object of the preposition.
    D.   Actually, it *is* the subject!

____ 15.   We know that some verbals can act as nouns. Which ones?
    A.   linking verbs and participles
    B.   gerunds and infinitives
    C.   participles and adverbs
    D.   subjunctives and conjunctives

____ 16.   What kind of verbal serves as one of the subjects in the
following sentence?
It's clear to me that recognizing verbals is an important
grammatical skill.
    A.   participle
    B.   gerund
    C.   infinitive
    D.   conjunctive

____ 17.   The preceding sentence has ____ subject(s) and ____ direct
object(s).
    A.   one…one
    B.   two…no
    C.   one…no
    D.   two…one

____ 18.   What kind of pronoun is *anybody?*
    A.   interrogative
    B.   limiting
    C.   relative
    D.   indefinite

____ 19.   How many nouns are in the following sentence?
He thought about the future as a place not a concept.
    A.   one
    B.   two
    C.   three
    D.   four

___ 20.   Why is the word *friendly* in the following sentence not a
           noun or a pronoun?
           He seems like a friendly person, don't you think?
           A. Actually, it *is* a noun!
           B. It's a descriptor—or a modifier—not a person, place,
               or thing.
           C. It can't be a noun because *friendly* is the subject of the
               sentence.
           D. It *is* a pronoun because *friendly* is a substitute for the
               noun *he.*

___ 21.   How many subjects are in the following sentence?
           The book that he wrote in 2002 is still a good introduction
           to web design.
           A. There is no subject—it's a fragment, not a complete
               sentence.
           B. one
           C. two
           D. three

22–26 Directions

Complete the following sentence by supplying an appropriate noun or
pronoun, as listed, for each blank.

_____ gave the _____ to the _____,
22. personal   23. common   24. common
    noun   noun   noun

_____ quickly ran into an alley _____ contained an
25. relative pronoun   26. relative pronoun

unmarked police car.

EXERCISE 10 • LEARNING TO LOVE ADJECTIVES

Purpose   To explore the descriptive and limiting talents of adjectives.

Reference   "When Words Collide" (9/e), Chapter 5

1–5 Directions

Underline all of the adjectives in these sentences. Below your underlinings, indicate whether the adjectives are descriptive (D) or limiting (L). If the adjective describes a subject noun connected to a linking verb, list it as a predicate adjective (pred. adj.).

Example The <u>weary</u> rescuers hiked <u>eight</u> miles to reach the <u>lost</u> hunter.
                    D   L   D

1.   I forgot to tell you that book is really long.

2.   Tom asked for three extensions, but the judge refused his loud request.

3.   The three boys were searching around the big house for their shoes, but their little sister hid them.

4.   The singer, suffering from stressed vocal chords, finally decided to cancel the sold-out concert.

5.   Concerned about her time, Marge worked on a steadier pace than in her last race.

6–10 Directions

In the space provided below each sentence, list all adjectives and indicate which words they modify. Also indicate the part of speech of each word that is modified.

Example You are fabulous; you are going to be a great success!
            Fabulous, a predicate adjective, modifies the pronoun *you.*
            Great, a descriptive adjective, modifies the noun *success.*

6. Anderson, who seemed rather shy at first, is the most talkative dentist I ever met.

7. That pie is the sweetest one of the five batches.

8. Five miles of strenuous hiking into that remote wilderness is no problem for me!

9. Twenty is my lucky number; which one is yours?

10. The lead singer had a bad habit of slipping off the stage.

11–20 Directions

Supply an adjective appropriate to the function indicated for each blank in these sentences.

Example _____ meeting won't result in a _____ outcome.
      (limiting)   (descriptive)

      This meeting won't result in a positive outcome.
      (limiting)   (descriptive)

11. A _____ truck hit a _____ barrier and rolled over.
    (limiting)   (descriptive)

12. Trust me: _____ option is not _____.
        (limiting)   (pred. adj.)

13. This has to be the _____ idea I've encountered in a
             (descriptive superlative)

  _____ time.
    (descriptive)

14. Harriet finally won the lottery on her _____ attempt.
                    (limiting)

15. Your _____ criteria for judging the contest are strangely _____.
    (limiting)   (pred. adj.)

16. _____ until the _____ crowd settled down, she
    (descriptive, as part   (descriptive)
    of a participial phrase)

    began to speak.

17. _____ time she tried to speak, the crowd hurled
    (limiting)

    _____ insults.
      (descriptive)

18. The _____, _____ vampire vanished quickly
      (descriptive)   (descriptive)

    into the _____ night.
        (descriptive)

19. Please give our _____ report to _____
           (descriptive)   (limiting)

    board member.

20. The rescue team was _____, _____ and _____
            (pred. adj.)   (pred. adj.)   (pred. adj.)

    after its _____ hours in the _____wilderness.
        (limiting)   (descriptive)

EXERCISE 11 • THOSE VERY INTERESTING ADVERBS

Purpose   To build recognition and use of adverbs.

Reference   "When Words Collide" (9/e), Chapter 5

1–15 Directions

Identify the part of speech of the underlined word in each of the
following sentences. Write the letter that corresponds to the correct
answer in the space at the left of each sentence.

_____ 1.   Coyote and Friends' new CD is <u>amazing</u>, don't you think?
             A. noun
             B. adjective
             C. adverb

_____ 2.   The robber ran out of the bank and <u>down</u> the street.
             A. adjective
             B. adverb
             C. preposition

_____ 3.   Baseball is fun, but basketball is <u>physically</u> more
             challenging.
             A. noun
             B. adverb
             C. conjunction

_____ 4.   The lieutenant ordered Gustavo and me to peel <u>5,000</u> potatoes.
             A. adverb
             B. pronoun
             C. adjective

_____ 5.   The bobcat ran <u>wildly</u> around its cage.
             A. adverb
             B. adjective
             C. interjection

_____ 6.   <u>This</u> option works for me.
             A. adjective
             B. pronoun
             C. adverb

_____ 7.   I <u>absolutely</u> will never be late for class again.
       A. adverb
       B. adjective
       C. conjunction

_____ 8.   I hope I never see <u>another</u> zucchini!
       A. adverb
       B. noun
       C. pronoun

_____ 9.   Our women's soccer team is <u>magnificent.</u>
       A. adjective
       B. adverb
       C. noun

_____ 10.   <u>Please</u> seat Meryl Streep next to me.
       A. preposition
       B. adverb
       C. conjunction

_____ 11.   <u>Prancing</u> merrily down the lane, she encountered the evil troll.
       A. adverb
       B. adjective
       C. noun

_____ 12.   <u>Now</u> it can be told!
       A. adverb
       B. preposition
       C. adjective

_____ 13.   Do you believe you are <u>well</u>-educated?
       A. adjective
       B. preposition
       C. adverb

_____ 14.   I am not convinced that Sara is smarter <u>than</u> he.
       A. conjunction
       B. adverb
       C. preposition

_____ 15.   Negotiations have broken down <u>between</u> labor and management.
       A. adverb
       B. preposition
       C. conjunction

16–25 Directions

The following questions ask you to identify adverbs correctly and to know how to use them properly in sentences. Select the correct answer from the choices provided.

___ 16.　What is the adverb in the following sentence?
　　　　Building the high-rise waterfront condominiums was more demanding than Werner had remembered from past projects.
　　　　A.　high-rise
　　　　B.　more
　　　　C.　remembered
　　　　D.　past

___ 17.　Which of the following choices is true about adverbs?
　　　　A.　They always appear before the word they modify.
　　　　B.　They always end in –ly.
　　　　C.　They never modify the subject of a sentence.
　　　　D.　They always indicate direction or place.

___ 18.　Which of the following underlined items is *not* an adverb?
　　　　A.　<u>definitively,</u> the smartest student
　　　　B.　a <u>really</u> bright student
　　　　C.　the <u>tallest</u> building on the block
　　　　D.　a <u>truly</u> principled decision

___ 19.　Which is the correct punctuation from the choices provided?
　　　　Heavy rains are delaying what is left of the grape harvest _____ clear weather is forecast for next week.
　　　　A.　, however,
　　　　B.　; however,

___ 20.　What is the adverb in the following sentence?
　　　　The store manager made an announcement over the loudspeaker that he planned to close the store earlier the day after Thanksgiving.
　　　　A.　made
　　　　B.　over
　　　　C.　earlier
　　　　D.　after

___ 21. In which sentence is the adverb used incorrectly?
  A. Sara hurriedly changed her plans before her boss changed his mind.
  B. She quit her job at the nursing home immediately after she won the high jump event.
  C. He thought eating 17 hot dogs in five minutes was a real good plan for earning $50.
  D. You know very well that I must have a late afternoon nap if I don't get my coffee early enough.

___ 22. In which sentence is the adverb *good* used correctly?
  A. The bread smells good.
  B. He whittled good.
  C. He felt good after two hours of yoga.
  D. After seven communications workshops, the council still doesn't run good.

___ 23. Adverbs generally answer all but the following.
  A. who
  B. when
  C. why
  D. how

___ 24. Which of the following uses correctly the superlative form of the adverb *cohesively?*
  A. Of all the proposals they considered, the first worked more cohesively.
  B. Of all the proposals they considered, the first worked most cohesively.
  C. Of all the proposals they considered, the first worked cohesivlier.
  D. Of all the proposals they considered, the first worked cohesivliest.

___ 25. Which of the following may an adverb *not* modify?
  A. a verb
  B. an adverb
  C. an adjective
  D. a noun

EXERCISE 12 • PREPOSITIONS: THE PARTS OF SPEECH
WITH A PREFERENCE FOR PHRASES

Purpose   To correctly identify prepositions, especially as parts
                     of phrases.

                     To understand the effect prepositional phrases have
                     on meaning.

Reference   "When Words Collide" (9/e), Chapter 5

1–13 Directions

Choose the correct response from the choices offered.

____ 1.   What is/are the prepositional phrase(s) in the following
           sentence?
           Maybe he should take something for seasickness before he
           gets on the ship.
           A.   take something for
           B.   for seasickness
           C.   on the ship
           D.   Both A and C
           E.   Both B and C

____ 2.   What is the first of the three prepositional phrases in the
           following sentence?
           The old stable, which had been built in the late 1800s over an
           inactive volcano, was burning quickly, to Salvatore's dismay.
           A.   in the late 1800s
           B.   was burning quickly
           C.   to Salvatore's dismay

____ 3.   Which of the following three sentences does *not* contain a
           preposition?
           A.   She started canning four years ago, testing her skill
                with some basic recipes for jams, dilly beans, relish and
                dried plums.
           B.   Once people start raising chickens, the logical next step
                is beekeeping.
           C.   If you stay here after the parade, you can collect the
                extra balloons.

____ 4.   How many prepositions are in this sentence?
He takes walks in shorts, rides to work on his tricycle and eats peanut butter with raspberry jam sandwiches for lunch.
A.   three
B.   four
C.   five
D.   six
E.   seven

5.   In question 4, what are the prepositional phrases? Write them here. Separate each one with a semicolon.

_____

_____

____ 6.   How many prepositions are in this sentence?
The stucco on the house is made from a mix of clay dug from the building site, then sifted and mixed with cow manure and nylon fiber.
A.   none
B.   one
C.   two
D.   three
E.   four

7.   In question 6, what are the prepositional phrases? Write them here. Separate each with a semicolon.

_____

_____

____ 8.   How many prepositions are in this sentence?
One of the ecology students wondered aloud in class whether there was any effect of biodegradable tableware on the environment.
A.   none
B.   one
C.   two
D.   three
E.   four

9. In question 8, what are the prepositional phrases? Write them here. Separate each with a period.

_____

_____

___ 10. How many prepositions are in this sentence?
She has been involved in studies on attention for decades, and has made significant contributions to understanding consciousness and memory.
A. none
B. one
C. two
D. three
E. four

11. In question 10, what are the prepositional phrases? Write them here. Separate each with a semicolon.

_____

_____

___ 12. IIow many prepositions are in this sentence?
He settled for a birdie on the 18th hole after missing an eagle chance from 10 feet.
A. none
B. one
C. two
D. three
E. four

13. In question 12, what are the prepositional phrases? Write them here. Separate each with a semicolon.

_____

_____

14–18 Directions

This section deals with proper placement of prepositional phrases. In the following sentences, confusions in meaning are caused by misplaced prepositional phrases. Rewrite the sentences with the prepositional phrases properly placed.

14. Finneman recently moved to San Francisco from Seattle, where he owned a magazine that focused on miniature golf competitions for 11 years.

_____

_____

15. The officer spotted the fleeing burglar hiding in the rose bush with his infrared goggles.

_____

_____

16. Janet entertained us with stories about a recent trip to New York in her Prius.

_____

_____

17. Krissy made some pasta for her niece with parmesan cheese.

_____

_____

18. He solved, in just 22 minutes, the crossword puzzle published on Sunday.
    (**Note:** Try to make this sentence more concise as you work on the alignment of these phrases.)

_____

_____

Bonus Question

Explain the difference between a prepositional phrase and a participial phrase. Then write a sentence containing an example of each. Circle and identify each of the phrase types.

_____

_____

_____

_____

_____

_____

_____

EXERCISE 13 • PREPOSITIONS VS. CONJUNCTIONS

Purpose   To build awareness of the specific role prepositions play in introducing phrases, compared with the role of conjunctions, which link words in phrases and clauses.

Reference   "When Words Collide" (9/e), Chapter 5

1–10 Directions

Circle the answer that correctly identifies the underlined portion, and then in the space provided, briefly explain how the part of speech functions in the sentence.

Example   I nabbed the last cookie in the jar, <u>but</u> my sister demanded half of it.

Answer   *But* is a coordinating conjunction. It joins the two independent clauses.

1.   I always schedule my physical therapy appointments <u>after</u> I've had my daily run.
     A.   preposition
     B.   coordinating conjunction
     C.   subordinating conjunction

     _____

     _____

2.   I can't believe <u>that</u> summer is almost over!
     A.   preposition
     B.   coordinating conjunction
     C.   subordinating conjunction

     _____

     _____

3. The coach was furious <u>when</u> his young protégé fell off the balance beam.
   A. preposition
   B. coordinating conjunction
   C. subordinating conjunction

   _____

   _____

4. <u>Despite</u> the bad sound system, the concert was one of the best of the year.
   A. preposition
   B. coordinating conjunction
   C. subordinating conjunction

   _____

   _____

5. James disappeared from the campground <u>without</u> a trace.
   A. preposition
   B. coordinating conjunction
   C. subordinating conjunction

   _____

   _____

6. At 5,000 feet, the mountaineer decided to return to camp <u>because he didn't have the proper equipment</u>.
   A. prepositional phrase
   B. dependent clause
   C. independent clause

   _____

   _____

7. <u>Following his crushing defeat</u>, the candidate retreated into the family business for two months.
   A. prepositional phrase
   B. dependent clause
   C. independent clause

   _____

   _____

8. The soccer team had an amazing win <u>within the last two exciting but bone-chilling minutes</u> of play.
   A. prepositional phrase
   B. dependent clause
   C. independent clause

   _____

   _____

9. He was presenting the final argument for his dissertation when he received the news <u>about his newborn baby</u>.
   A. prepositional phrase
   B. dependent clause
   C. independent clause

   _____

   _____

10. When he handed in his homework, <u>he forgot to give the teacher the last page</u>.
    A. prepositional phrase
    B. dependent clause
    C. independent clause

    _____

    _____

11–15 Directions

Choose the answer that correctly identifies the number of prepositions or clauses in the sentences that follow.

___ 11. How many prepositions are in the following sentence? No one could successfully dissuade him from surfing for seven hours straight on his vacations.
   A. none
   B. one
   C. two
   D. three
   E. four

____ 12. How many prepositions are in the following sentence?
The teacher and her guest speaker walked into the classroom, greeted the students, and handed out pamphlets on the study abroad program.
A. none
B. one
C. two
D. three
E. four

____ 13. How many clauses are in the following sentence?
Not taking the medicine as prescribed could allow the infection to re-establish itself in your body and become more resistant to the drugs later.
A. one
B. two
C. three
D. four
E. five

____ 14. How many clauses are in the following sentence?
Jerry polished the trophy that sat in the bowling alley case an hour before every tournament.
A. one
B. two
C. three
D. four
E. five

____ 15. How many prepositions and clauses are in the following sentence?
The legislation you are proposing for the new budget is worthwhile and needed, but I'm afraid we won't have the votes to pass it in the remaining weeks of the current legislative session.
A. one preposition, one clause
B. two prepositions, two clauses
C. three prepositions, two clauses
D. two prepositions, three clauses
E. three prepositions, four clauses

Bonus Question 1

Rewrite the sentence so that a preposition is used to create a more streamlined sentence with a clearer meaning.

His expertise will help shed light on the issues debated by the city government surrounding the use of Tasers.

_____

_____

_____

Bonus Question 2

Rewrite the sentence so that a preposition is used to create a more streamlined sentence with a clearer meaning.

I am writing an article pertaining to a public policy proposal on child health care, and I was wondering whether you would be available for an interview.

_____

_____

_____

NAME _____   SCORE _____

EXERCISE 14 • COMPARATIVES AND SUPERLATIVES

Purpose   To continue to build understanding of parts of speech, pronoun use and the specific role the preposition *than* plays in defining sentences of comparisons (objective pronouns), while the conjunction *than* is linked to subjective pronouns.

To correctly identify the proper part of speech for expressing the degree of a superlative.

To distinguish between the use of *then* as an adverb and *than*.

Reference   "When Words Collide" (9/e), Chapter 5

Directions   Circle the correct choice in each of the following sentences. On the line underneath, write the part of speech of the circled word, or if a question is asked, provide an answer.

1. Let's go to the movie first, (A. then B. than) get some pizza.

   _____

2. Are you sure Nancy is a better fundraiser than (A. her B. she)?

   _____

3. No one is denying that she is more careful than (A. I B. me).

   _____

4. I'd rather eat a doughnut covered in ants (A. than B. then) submit to your criticism about my fashion sense.

   _____

5. Why is "she" in the following sentence correct?
   Believe me, no one is smarter than <u>she</u> when it comes to calculus.
   A. The preposition <u>than</u> tells us that there is no need for the nominative case.
   B. "smarter" as a comparative adjective requires an extended comparison, as in "than she is smart...."
   C. "she" is properly used as the object of the preposition <u>than</u>.
   D. None of the above is correct.

6. I still believe Harold is funnier than (A. she B. her).

_____

7. My roommates say that I'm much neater than (A. they B. them).

_____

8. Tami hung up the phone, and (A. than B. then), only one hour later, the package arrived in her mailbox!

_____

9. My father always said that my mother was a better driver than (A. him B. he).

_____

10. His condition was (A. much worser B. much worse) than doctors had expected.

_____

   What part of speech is *much* in the above sentence?

_____

11. Your chocolate muffins taste better (A. than any B. than any others) I've eaten.

_____

12. Give a reason for your answer in question 11. Why is your choice correct and the other answer incorrect? What is the difference in meaning?

_____

_____

_____

_____

_____

13. (A. More often B. More oftener) than not, we find online introductions can create misunderstandings and be awkward.

_____

14. She complained that her salary and benefits were lower than (A. her assistant B. her assistant's).

_____

15. Give a reason for your answer in item 14. Why is your choice correct and the other answer incorrect? What is the difference in meaning?

_____

_____

_____

_____

_____

EXERCISE 15 • CHECKUP: VERBS, VERBALS, MODIFIERS

Purpose   To strengthen your understanding and use of verbs,
              verbals and modifiers in effective writing.

Reference   "When Words Collide" (9/e), Chapters 4 and 5

1–5 Directions

Select the correct response from the choices offered.

___ 1.   Identify the verb or verbs in the following sentence.
          Practicing her downhill ski routine every day gave Lindsay
          the confidence to join the ski team and to eventually win an
          Olympic medal.
          A. practicing, gave
          B. gave, win
          C. win
          D. gave

___ 2.   What kind of verb or verbs is (are) in sentence 1? (Circle all
          that apply)
          A. transitive
          B. intransitive
          C. linking

___ 3.   What kind of verbals are there in sentence 1?
          A. participle and gerund
          B. gerund and infinitives
          C. infinitives and participle
          D. There are no verbals in sentence 1.

___ 4.   What kind of verb is in the following sentence?
          Stop!
          A. transitive
          B. intransitive
          C. linking
          D. It's not a sentence.

___ 5.   A linking verb can never have a _____ .
          A. pronoun as a predicate nominative
          B. a past tense
          C. direct object
          D. predicate adjective

6–10 Directions

In the spaces provided, supply appropriate modifiers as identified below the line.

6. Jerry said he is "_____ excited" about his new job and that he
    (adverb)

    is _____ looking forward to some new challenges.
      (adverb)

7. _____ company has grown _____ in the last
    (possessive pronoun)   (adverb)

    _____ years.
    (limiting adjective)

8. Her reputation as a _____ columnist is _____.
          (descriptive adjective)   (compound modifier—
                                       adverb and adjective)

9. _____, she was struck by a speeding motorcycle.
    (participial phrase as an adjective)

10. After a _____ summer in Arizona, he moved to more
       (descriptive adjective)

    _____ Oregon.
    (descriptive adjective)

11–15 Directions

Replace the following underlined phrases with one strong, descriptive verb.

Example instead of: <u>stare at angrily</u> **glare**

11. instead of: <u>look at sullenly</u>   _____

12. instead of: <u>walk heavily and laboriously</u>   _____

13. instead of: <u>enthusiastically give praise to</u>   _____

14. instead of: <u>constantly complain</u>   _____

15. instead of: <u>weep intensely and loudly</u>   _____

16–18 Directions

The following sentences contain two clauses. Use the information in one of the clauses to create a verbal, so that the resulting sentence is more concise—as a simple sentence with only one clause. Underline your verbal and identify its type.

Example   Tom was running to class; however, he tripped and fell.
Revised   <u>Running to class</u>, Tom tripped and fell. *participial phrase*

16. Tom builds model planes from balsa wood, and this is his favorite hobby.

_____

17. One of the pledges that she gave her constituents is that she will decrease the sales tax very soon.

_____

18. The defendant said he will go to jail, but that he will constantly maintain his innocence while there.

_____

EXERCISE 16 • SUBJECTS, VERBS AND OBJECTS

Purpose   To develop mastery of sentence components through accurate identification of sentence subjects, verbs and objects, in all their forms: direct, indirect, objects of prepositions, predicate nominatives and predicate adjectives.

Reference   "When Words Collide" (9/e), Chapters 4 and 5

Directions   Select the correct answer from the options provided, or fill in the blanks or underline as instructed.

___ 1.   What are the only two parts of speech that can serve as the subject of a sentence?
A.   nouns and pronouns
B.   nouns and gerunds
C.   nouns and adverbs
D.   pronouns and verbs

___ 2.   What is the direct object in the following sentence?
Before the surgery, Ceresse gave her daughter a big hug.
A.   surgery
B.   Ceresse
C.   daughter
D.   hug

3.   Sentence 2 contains two other grammatical "objects." List them below according to their grammatical terms.

Indirect object _____

Object of preposition _____

___ 4.   What is the direct object in the following sentence?
Jill generously offered two chocolates to her sister for failing the driving test.
A.   Jill
B.   chocolates
C.   sister
D.   test

___ 5.   Why does the preceding sentence have a direct object? Because the main clause has:
A.   a transitive verb
B.   an intransitive verb
C.   a linking verb
D.   a helping (auxiliary) verb

_____ 6.   What is the subject of the following sentence?
There is only one place left on my bucket list to visit: Paris.
A.   There
B.   place
C.   bucket list
D.   Paris

_____ 7.   What is the subject of the following sentence?
According to anonymous sources, two-thirds of all jelly
bean shipments out of Oregon include a half green, half
yellow and one half black, half orange bean.
A.   anonymous sources
B.   two-thirds
C.   jelly bean shipments
D.   Oregon

_____ 8.   The verb in sentence 7 is _include._ What kind of verb is it?
A.   transitive
B.   linking
C.   intransitive
D.   It's not a verb; it's a gerund.

_____ 9.   How many subjects are in the following sentence?
Large predators who live at the edge of civilization
sometimes make foraging trips into nearby urban or
suburban neighbors.
A.   one
B.   two
C.   three
D.   none

_____ 10.   Same question for this sentence.
Right there, lying on the table, is your ticket for your
vacation in Bali.
A.   none
B.   one
C.   two
D.   three

_____ 11.   By the way, what kind of verb is that in question 10?
A.   transitive
B.   intransitive
C.   linking

___ 12. How many subjects are in the following sentence?
Wishing he'd brought his umbrella for the dark skies and shocking storms.
A. None. It's a fragment, not a complete sentence.
B. It may be a fragment, but it still has one subject.
C. It *is* a complete sentence, with one subject.
D. It has two subjects.

___ 13. Why is *hail* in the following sentence not its subject?
The downpour of hail sounded an eerie, symphonic melody.
A. It is the direct object.
B. It is the indirect object.
C. It is the object of the preposition.
D. Actually, it *is* the subject!

___ 14. Which verbal—or verbals—can be the subject of a sentence?
A. participles
B. gerunds
C. infinitives
D. Both B and C are correct.

___ 15. What do we call the underlined word in the following sentence?
It's clear to me that recognizing verbals is an important grammatical <u>skill</u>.
A. direct object
B. indirect object
C. linking verb
D. predicate nominative

___ 16. There are two verbs in the preceding exercise sentence.
They are both
A. transitive
B. fragmentary
C. intransitive
D. linking

___ 17. What grammatical term suggests a "mirror reflection" of a sentence's subject?
A. indirect object
B. predicate nominative
C. direct object
D. gerund

___ 18. What is the complete direct object of the following sentence?
I simply can't believe your story.
A. believe
B. can't believe
C. the project
D. your story

____ 19.　　Underline and mark all the subjects, verbs and objects in the following sentence, indicating the kind of verbs and objects as well.
The waitress took the patrons their order, but they complained she wasn't fast enough and walked out.

____ 20.　　What is the verb in the following sentence?
Training for three months and sacrificing almost everything for a chance to qualify for the 2016 Olympics.
A.　training
B.　sacrificing
C.　qualify
D.　The sentence does not contain a verb.

21–25 Directions

Complete the following sentence by supplying an appropriate word for each blank.

_____ gave the _____ to the _____,
21. subject　　　　　　　　22. direct object　　　23. object of preposition

_____ seemed _____ to receive it.
24. subject　　　　　　　25. predicate adjective

EXERCISE 17 • VERBALS REVISITED: AS PHRASES AND SENTENCE ELEMENTS

Purpose   To correctly identify verbal phrases.

To understand the role of a phrase as a part of speech and, at times, a sentence element.

Reference   "When Words Collide" (9/e), Chapters 4, 5 and 6

1–10 Directions

In the spaces provided under each sentence, write the type of verbal phrase, the complete verbal phrase, its part of speech and its use in the sentence as a sentence element, if appropriate.

Example   She decided never to follow the crowd.

Infinitive: *to follow the crowd.* Noun, operating as the direct object of the verb *decided*

1.   Everyone knew the officer running toward the house couldn't do a thing to stop the explosion.

     _____

     _____

2.   Skateboarding was easier in town after they built a dedicated park.

     _____

     _____

3.   The gold miner, frustrated by the lack of gold, quit his search shortly after noon.

     _____

     _____

4. All Bill ever wanted was to sing the national anthem at a football game.

    _____

    _____

5. Mark decided attending graduate school was his best shot at a new career.

    _____

    _____

6. He often exclaimed that working in a factory was a hard way to earn a living.

    _____

    _____

7. Sam supports the initiative to ban smoking in all enclosed public places.

    _____

    _____

8. Waiting for the boring lecture to end, the boy blew spitballs at the speaker.

    _____

    _____

9. The coach's plan seems like the best opportunity to help the team.

    _____

    _____

10. Alicia learned algebra watching "Sesame Street."

    _____

    _____

EXERCISE 18 • INDEPENDENT AND DEPENDENT CLAUSES

Purpose   To learn how to identify and construct effective
                   clauses by recognizing the differences between
                   phrases and clauses.

Reference   "When Words Collide" (9/e), Chapter 3 (Types of
                   Sentences); Chapter 5 (Conjunctions)

1–5 Directions

Examine each sentence and respond to each question below by selecting
the correct option.

_____ 1.   What kind of clause is *that there are plenty of parks to visit*
            in this sentence?
            Driving around Captiva Island showed me that there are
            plenty of parks to visit.
            A.   independent
            B.   dependent
            C.   insubordinate
            D.   It's not a clause; it's a participial phrase.

_____ 2.   How many clauses and how many phrases are in sentence 1?
            A.   one and none
            B.   one and one
            C.   two and none
            D.   two and three

_____ 3.   Fill in the blanks.
            An independent clause must have a _____ and must
            contain a _____.
            A.   modifier…subordinate meaning
            B.   verb…predicate nominative
            C.   subject…direct object
            D.   verb…complete thought

_____ 4.   How many prepositional phrases are in the following
            sentence?
            Pushing his diplomatic intentions, the president waved to the
            admiral and signaled for the vice president to do the same.
            A.   none
            B.   one
            C.   two
            D.   three

_____ 5.   What is the subject of the independent clause in sentence 4?
          A.   intentions
          B.   president
          C.   admiral
          D.   vice president

6–10 Directions

Underline the complete independent clause(s) in each sentence.

Example   The fire that destroyed the Sherwood Apartments has been confirmed as arson.

Answer   <u>The fire</u> that destroyed the Sherwood Apartments <u>has been confirmed as arson.</u>

(In this example, note that a dependent clause separates the subject of the main [independent] clause from its verb and following phrase.)

6.   Against my better judgment, I am recommending we participate in this investment club.

7.   The fire that struck Stickton Warehouses last night destroyed three buildings and injured six people.

8.   My brother tried to sneak out of the house last summer, but the neighbors called the police because they thought he was a burglar.

9.   The island was filled with many winding trails, small lakes, and herds of dangerous wild pigs.

10. Do you know that walnuts can be used to touch up wooden furniture scratches?

11–15 Directions

Combine each pair of sentences into one, creating a sentence that contains a main (independent) and a subordinate (dependent) clause. Such a combination shows that the independent clause you choose will be the main part of the sentence, and the dependent clause will be secondary.

After you write the sentence, underline the dependent clause. In some cases, you may want to incorporate a phrase into the sentence, depending on the amount of information included. This is an opportunity to create more concise sentences.

Example   Dan lost the TweetMeHoney account. It was because the agency didn't provide adequate research support.

Rewrite   Dan lost the TweetMeHoney account <u>because the agency didn't provide proper research support.</u>

11. An airline passenger went through a secured door at JFK airport Tuesday morning, and this caused the Transportation Security Agency to shut down the terminal. This delayed flights for more than five hours.

_____

_____

_____

12. Rescue workers removed 10 tons of rock from the shaft. Then they drilled a secondary tunnel through five feet of rock, and then they found the trapped miners.

_____

_____

_____

13. The district attorney gave his summation to the jury this morning, but he appeared agitated and also confused while doing so. His name is Frank Anderson.

_____

_____

_____

14. The analysts' conclusions were original and thought-provoking. However, none of the board members agreed with them.

_____

_____

_____

15. The books are lying on the table. They must be returned to the library today.

_____

_____

_____

16–20 Directions

Using the information provided, create one complete sentence according to the sentence type indicated. In some cases, you will use both phrases and clauses to use all the information. Underline the independent clause or clauses for each sentence you create.

Example	Write a compound sentence using the following information: There was an election Tuesday in the city of Circleville. In that election, city voters approved a bond issue to build a new fire station. However, they rejected a bond issue for a new convention center.
Answer	Circleville voters Tuesday approved a bond issue to build a new fire station, but they rejected a bond issue for a new convention center. (two independent clauses joined by the coordinating conjunction *but*)

16. Write a simple sentence with this information: Heavy rains hit Circleville last night. That rain was mixed with hail, and that combination made for dangerous driving.

_____

_____

_____

17. Write a complex sentence with this information: Striking machinists will return to work tomorrow. They agreed tonight to do so. They have been on the picket lines for three months.

_____

_____

_____

18. Write a compound sentence with this information: The women's basketball team of Bentley College was seeking its ninth straight victory. However, it lost to Conan College in overtime by a score of 88–87.

_____

_____

_____

19. Write a compound-complex sentence (at least two independent clauses, with at least one dependent clause) with this information: I used to love airline travel. However, I prefer to use the train now. That's because it is more hassle-free.

_____

_____

_____

20. Write a simple sentence with this information: Henderson County Food Bank volunteers did the following in an eight-hour period today: They packaged more than 500 school lunch packs. They also delivered 200 hot meals to homebound senior citizens. In addition, they stored more than 1,000 canned goods from donors.

_____

_____

_____

EXERCISE 19 • THAT/WHICH/WHO AND RESTRICTIVE/NONRESTRICTIVE CONSTRUCTIONS

Purpose   To learn the difference between restrictive and
                   nonrestrictive constructions.

                   To choose correct relative pronouns and punctuation
                   for them.

Reference   "When Words Collide" (9/e), Chapters 6 and 7

PART ONE: RESTRICTIVE OR NONRESTRICTIVE?

1–15 Directions

Identify the underlined section according to the following code.

        A   = restrictive clause
        B   = nonrestrictive clause
        C   = restrictive phrase
        D   = nonrestrictive phrase

____ 1.   Billy, <u>who has been struggling with his writing</u>, hopes that
           his creative bursts will excuse any literary shortcomings.

____ 2.   Sara's novel, <u>which received the Chattanooga Book Award
           in 2004</u>, is in its ninth printing.

____ 3.   The leaves <u>rustling in the trees</u> slowly started to fall.

____ 4.   His digital animation process, <u>patented only two years ago</u>,
           is being eagerly sought by all the major studios.

____ 5.   Every spring, Harold, <u>a failed efficiency expert</u>, moves all
           the boxes and trunks from one side of the attic to the other.

____ 6.   Crossing the finish line, she realized <u>she had achieved her
           lifelong dream</u>.

____ 7.   Helen, <u>the new account executive</u>, walked into the meeting
           room and gave a dazzling presentation.

____ 8.   The violinmaker made five trips to Italy in one year <u>after
           becoming obsessed with the violins made by 16th century
           craftsmen</u>.

___ 9.   Choose the sentence <u>that includes an error</u>.

___ 10.   Sarah's etiquette newsletter, <u>which is being distributed across the country</u>, is being hailed as a "triumph in civility."

___ 11.   The judges <u>seated at the table</u> were laughing and joking.

___ 12.   The hostage <u>who managed to escape</u> lost twenty pounds in her trek across the mountains.

___ 13.   The students learned <u>they can mount a well-organized campaign.</u>

___ 14.   Sara, <u>drained by several hours of exams</u>, collapsed in bed.

___ 15.   The device <u>triggering the explosion</u> is from a company in Idaho.

PART TWO: THE TROUBLE WITH *THAT!*

16–20 Directions

The word *that* can be used three ways: as a limiting adjective, as a conjunction and as a relative pronoun. Using structure as your guide, identify the part of speech for the use of *that* in the following sentences.

___ 16.   Toledo police released the official transcript of the witness' statement about the Hollywood Avenue riots that took place last month.
   A. conjunction
   B. adjective
   C. relative pronoun

___ 17.   That donut was the first one I'd eaten in three months.
   A. conjunction
   B. adjective
   C. relative pronoun

___ 18.   The book that I recommend is an easy introduction to playing chess.
   A. conjunction
   B. adjective
   C. relative pronoun

____ 19.   Brendan won the spelling bee the second year in a row with
          uncooperative, a word that he first learned during his
          "Terrible Twos."
          A. conjunction
          B. adjective
          C. relative pronoun

____ 20.   I forgot to tell you that this is a nonrefundable purchase.
          A. conjunction
          B. adjective
          C. relative pronoun

PART THREE

21–30 Directions

Select the correct pronoun (with appropriate punctuation and subject–
verb agreement) from the choices offered.

____ 21.   Web designs _____ win awards often lack complicated
          features.
          A. that
          B. which

____ 22.   Diane _____ is a motivational speaker by trade.
          A. , that has become a tireless advocate for the homeless,
          B. that has become a tireless advocate for the homeless
          C. , who has become a tireless advocate for the homeless,
          D. who has become a tireless advocate for the homeless

____ 23.   Are you sending this package of news clippings _____ to
          Boise?
          A. , that has been sitting here and gathering dust for two
              weeks,
          B. which has been sitting here and gathering dust for two
              weeks
          C. , which has been sitting here and gathering dust for
              two weeks,
          D. that has been sitting here and gathering dust for two weeks

____ 24.   As more water is exposed to sunlight, more heat is stored in
          the water, _____ warms and melts some of the ice.
          A. that
          B. which

____ 25.   An export slowdown _____ is contributing to the shutdown of factories in several countries.
    A.   , which has been magnified by the global financial crisis,
    B.   that has been magnified by the global financial crisis
    C.   which has been magnified by the global financial crisis

____ 26.   What is your opinion of the commentary _____ was published in our neighborhood newsletter?
    A.   that
    B.   which

____ 27.   Stock certificates _____ are counterfeit.
    A.   that have a pink watermark
    B.   which have a pink watermark
    C.   , which have a pink watermark,

____ 28.   The protesters _____ refused to disperse have been arrested and jailed.
    A.   that
    B.   who
    C.   whom

____ 29.   The CEO's budget plan, _____ foresees near-record deficits just ahead, is sure to meet resistance by the board.
    A.   that
    B.   who
    C.   which

____ 30.   She is a well-known scholar _____ understands academic commitment.
    A.   who
    B.   that
    C.   which

PART FOUR

31–34 Directions

Using the information presented below, write four sentences: one with a nonrestrictive clause, one with a restrictive clause and two with a nonrestrictive appositive phrase.

Diabetic acidosis is a life-threatening condition. It can occur in people with type 1 diabetes. Type 2 diabetics also can get it, but it's less common with them. Diabetic acidosis is referred to by doctors as *ketoacidosis*. Ketoacidosis is caused when insulin is deficient or lacking. A lack of insulin leads to high blood sugar levels and the presence of what are known as *ketones* in the blood and also the urine. Ketones are byproducts or waste products; they are produced when the body burns fat for energy. And then there is a build-up of acids. The build-up is of certain acids. Those acids are called *ketoacids*.

31. Sentence with a nonrestrictive clause:

_____

_____

_____

32. Sentence with a restrictive clause:

_____

_____

_____

33. Sentence with an appositive phrase:

_____

_____

_____

34. Sentence with an appositive phrase:

_____

_____

_____

EXERCISE 20 • APPOSITIVES

Purpose	To improve understanding and use of appositives in your writing.
Reference	"When Words Collide" (9/e), Chapters 6 and 7
Note	Pay particular attention to how appositives (used as single words, phrases or clauses) can add helpful, complementary information to a sentence. Note also the importance of proper punctuation and pronoun case in their use.

1–10 Directions

Select the correct answer from the choices offered.

____ 1.   What is the appositive in the following sentence?
Harriet Thompson, editor of the new Browning Book series, will speak to our students this afternoon at three o'clock.
    A. Harriet
    B. Thompson
    C. editor
    D. series

____ 2.   What is the appositive in the following sentence?
Tommy's aunt, Sarajean, often tells the story of coming to America with her sisters.
    A. aunt
    B. Sarajean
    C. story
    D. America

____ 3.   In the previous sentence, why is there a comma after _aunt_ and _Sarajean?_
    A. _Sarajean_ is a restrictive construction, denoting a particular aunt.
    B. Appositives are always set off with commas.
    C. _Sarajean_ is used in a nonrestrictive or looser sense.
    D. It is obvious that Tommy has more than one aunt, and it is likely that more than one aunt tells this story.
    E. Both C and D are correct.

____ 4. Is the appositive in the following sentence a phrase or a clause?
Jared Sumpter, president of Tri-County chemicals, declined comment about the pending toxic waste litigation.
A. phrase
B. clause

____ 5. Is the appositive in the following sentence a phrase or a clause?
Wendy Bowman, soon to be appointed chair of the United Way Board, has an inspirational life story.
A. phrase
B. clause

____ 6. Is the appositive in the following sentence a phrase or a clause?
The paper wrote a glowing story about Billy Andersen, who will be honored as Smallville's "First Citizen" tonight.
A. phrase
B. clause

____ 7. Identify the appropriate pronoun to use in the following sentence and whether, based on meaning, punctuation is necessary.
The company decided that the three of us, Sara, Henry and _____ will represent it at the conference.
A. me,
B. I,
C. me
D. I

____ 8. Name the two nouns that are followed by two nearby appositives in the following sentence.
One of the largest calderas in the world, Ngorogoro, is in Tanzania, a republic in East Africa.
A. calderas…Ngorogoro
B. world…Ngorogoro
C. calderas…republic
D. calderas…Tanzania

____ 9. Does the following sentence contain an appositive? Why or why not?
Steve Martin is a comedian as well as a great banjo player.
A. Yes. *Comedian* and *banjo player* complement and add helpful information to the subject, *Steve Martin.*
B. Not really. The nouns *comedian* and *banjo player* follow the linking verb *is,* which makes them a predicate noun (or nominative).
C. *Banjo player* would be an appositive if *as well as* was preceded by a comma.

____ 10. Why is there no comma after the subject in the following sentence?

The man who died of lung cancer smoked three packs of cigarettes a day.

A. The *who* clause specifies or clarifies the noun *man,* which makes this a restrictive clause and a restrictive appositive.

B. Commas are not needed in a short sentence.

C. Placing a comma after the subject *man* will harm the sentence's meter.

D. Both A and B are correct.

11–15 Directions

From the information provided, combine each pair of sentences into one by turning one clause into an appositive phrase. Underline the appositive phrase in your answer. Try to make your sentences as concise as possible.

Example George Mallory was a famous British explorer. He disappeared in 1924 during a climb of Mount Everest during the winter.

Rewrite George Mallory, a famous British explorer, disappeared in 1924 during a winter climb of Mount Everest.

11. Michael Jordan is a famous basketball player. He is now part owner of a team.

_____

_____

12. The *Kensington Review* is an annual publication, published by the Kensington Foundation. Today, it was announced that, immediately, the *Review* will cease publication.

_____

_____

13. Police say the suspect in the robbery of the First National Bank has been identified and arrested. He has been identified as Norman Bates, and he has been charged with the crime of first-degree robbery.

_____

_____

14. Cleveland is an important part of the region's history of manufacturing. That region has often been referred to as the "Rust Belt."

_____

_____

15. First-degree robbery is a felony. In many states, it is punishable by a prison term of 10 years, at a minimum.

_____

_____

Bonus Question

Write a sentence in which an appositive phrase relates to the object of a preposition rather than to a subject or a direct object. Underline the object of the preposition.

_____

_____

_____

_____

_____

_____

EXERCISE 21 • CASE 1

Purpose   To create consistency within sentences by using the correct case of pronouns.

Reference   "When Words Collide" (9/e), Chapter 6

Directions   Select the correct pronoun choice in each of the following sentences.

____ 1.   This is a great opportunity for him and _____.
A. I
B. me

____ 2.   Adding Sara and _____ to the members list of the ski club allowed us to get a group rate.
A. I
B. me

____ 3.   The woman _____ police believed committed the robbery has been released on bail.
A. who
B. whom

____ 4.   She is a highly-regarded scientist _____ has learned to accommodate many divergent theories.
A. who
B. whom

____ 5.   There is absolutely no way I will continue to put up with _____ incessant talking.
A. you're
B. your

____ 6.   _____ judges were unimpressed by the new line of clothing designed by the celebrity's father.
A. Us
B. We

____ 7.   Seriously, I don't think the prosecution has proven _____ case.
A. its
B. it's

___ 8.   Between you and _____ , I don't understand the point
          of this exercise.
          A. I
          B. me

___ 9.   _____ is the worst case of poison ivy I've ever seen.
          A. yours
          B. your's

___ 10.   It's quite apparent to _____ writers that this poetry
          competition is rigged.
          A. we
          B. us

___ 11.   The radio station is giving an award to _____ calls first.
          A. who
          B. whoever
          C. whom
          D. whomever

___ 12.   The court released the accused man despite what many
          thought was overwhelming evidence against _____ .
          A. his
          B. him

___ 13a.   I asked her to provide me the citation for the research that
          shows children (A. who B. whom) have been overprotected
          often

___ 13b.   become adults for (A. who B. whom) life is difficult outside
          the family circle.

___ 14.   That's not mine; it's _____ .
          A. yours.
          B. yours'.
          C. your's.

___ 15.   The Society of Jokesters decided to cancel _____ next
          meeting.
          A. their
          B. they're
          C. it's
          D. its

___ 16.   Say, _____ a blue moon out tonight!
          A. theirs
          B. they'res
          C. there's

____ 17.   I know it's hard _____ knowing I'm never coming back.
- A. you
- B. your

____ 18.   The county commission will soon release _____ traffic survey results.
- A. their
- B. they're
- C. it's
- D. its

____ 19.   _____ going to tell her she's got a spider in her hair?
- A. Who's
- B. Whose

____ 20.   Did you know _____ building manager is a former Olympiad?
- A. their
- B. they're
- C. there

____ 21.   Don't you agree that _____ freelance writers should form a guild?
- A. us
- B. we

____ 22.   So, _____ up first?
- A. who's
- B. whose

____ 23.   This is mine; which is _____?
- A. ours
- B. our's
- C. ours'

____ 24.   _____ going to be very sorry if you eat that foot-long hot dog!
- A. Your
- B. You're

____ 25.   I'm going to vote for _____ tells the funniest joke.
- A. whoever
- B. whomever

____ 26.   It's official — the lottery winnings are _____!
- A. your's
- B. yours
- C. you'res

___ 27.　I certainly understand _____ asserting his Fifth
　　　　Amendment rights.
　　　　A.　him
　　　　B.　his

___ 28.　The other delegates and _____ immediately accepted
　　　　the resolution drafted by the Senate.
　　　　A.　him
　　　　B.　he

___ 29.　I look forward to _____ returning my call soon.
　　　　A.　you
　　　　B.　your

___ 30.　Writing the essay was challenging, but there were many
　　　　students _____ felt a sense of satisfaction and that
　　　　finishing made them more self-confident.
　　　　A.　who
　　　　B.　whom

EXERCISE 22 • CASE 2

Purpose   To continue to build an understanding of the proper
                     use of case and to improve editing abilities.

Reference   "When Words Collide" (9/e), Chapters 6

Directions   In each of the following sentences, correct all errors in
                     pronoun case, pronoun selection and noun
                     possessives. Make your edits at the sentence line or
                     just below. Watch for improper use of subject–verb
                     contractions and possessives (including those for
                     nouns). If the sentence is correct, write *Correct* in the
                     space below.

1.   Either of these lunch specials are a good deal.

2.   Do you think that sending Colin and she to the therapist is an idea
      who's time has come?

3.   Between you and I, this assignment is going to be difficult for we
      writers.

4.   Well, it's certainly someone's fault!

5.   The teacher will reward whomever he thinks will do the best job.

6.   You going to Hawaii on vacation has it's pluses and minuses.

7.   Theres a beautiful moon out tonight; its the kind of evening that
      remains in ones' heart.

8.   The puppy in that car is the one whom dug holes in my Mom's
      flowerbed.

9. She's much smarter than me, but our's is still a competitive relationship.

10. She and Tom's advocacy has been influential in improving childrens' safety.

11. He is the only one of the students who take the extra study sessions seriously.

12. Their's is a compelling explanation of those poems meanings.

13. Neither of these men could handle this crisis by themselves'.

14. Its just a matter of time until the finger of suspicion is pointed at we professional lobbyist's.

15. Who did the students choose to be the class president?

16. The group of screaming demonstrators were blocking the road which leads to the courthouse.

17. Shes afraid that the court will reject the attorney generals opinion.

18. Police have arrested a man that they say is responsible for a series

19. of fires in the citys' urban renewal district. There lead came from

20. an anonymous witness' phone call.

21. This is neither yours nor ours; it's theirs.

22. Your never going to believe who called today!

EXERCISE 23 • CHECKUP: PHRASES AND CLAUSES

Purpose   To assess your understanding of phrases and clauses, as well as your understanding of sentence construction.

Reference   "When Words Collide" (9/e), Chapters 3 through 7

Directions   Select the correct answer from the choices offered.

____ 1.   A participial phrase is always what part of speech?
      A. noun
      B. verb
      C. adverb
      D. adjective

____ 2.   A sentence fragment cannot stand alone as a complete thought. Which of the following three constructions is a fragment?
      A. Not only is this proposal going to fail, but it will do so miserably.
      B. All around the mulberry bush, with the monkey chasing the weasel.
      C. Wait!

____ 3.   Identify and describe the underlined section in the following sentence.
      To be happy <u>is to live well</u>.
      A. It's an infinitive phrase serving as the subject of the sentence.
      B. It's an infinitive phrase serving as the predicate nominative of the sentence.
      C. It's an infinitive clause.
      D. It's a gerund phrase serving as the direct object of the sentence.

____ 4.   A sentence fragment _____.
      A. never contains a subject or verb
      B. may contain a clause, but it does not express a complete thought
      C. never contains any punctuation
      D. is always a phrase

___ 5.   A gerund phrase, which can be the subject or direct object of a sentence, is always what part of speech?
    A. noun
    B. pronoun
    C. verb
    D. adjective

___ 6.   The following sentence seems to take forever to get to the point. What is the most precise explanation why?
    Although he had prepared intensely in the past two weeks, which actually caused him to fall ill, Smith, who had expected to win the competition easily, placed last in the national finals.
    A. Actually, it's not a sentence; it's a fragment, which explains the problem.
    B. The subordinate clause is buried in a pile of dependent clauses.
    C. Passive voice is the obvious culprit.
    D. Oversubordination is the problem: The independent (main) clause is interrupted by a host of dependent clauses.

___ 7.   What is the appropriate term for the underlined section in the following sentence?
    Does Rick plan <u>to attend every game</u> that the Ducks play next year?
    A. prepositional phrase
    B. infinitive clause
    C. subordinate clause
    D. infinitive phrase

___ 8.   How many clauses are in the following sentence?
    Between the Industrial Revolution of the late 18th century and the cleanliness movement of the early 20th century, reformers began promoting stringent standards of household conformity and order to the expanding middle class as examples of good citizenship and high morals.
    A. one
    B. two
    C. three
    D. none

___ 9.   The underlined section in the following sentence is called a(n) _____ clause.
    Sudhofter High, <u>which is home to two baseball teams</u>, has rarely seen its team in the regionals.
    A. independent clause
    B. nonrestrictive clause
    C. gerund phrase
    D. essential clause

____ 10. Identify the participial phrases in the following sentence. Completing her second triathlon in two weeks proved that Rebecca, though hampered by a shoulder injury, could overcome incredible obstacles.
 A. Completing her second triathlon
 B. hampered by a shoulder injury
 C. overcome incredible obstacles
 D. Both A and B are correct.

____ 11. How many dependent clauses are in the following sentence? He waited all morning for the mysterious stranger, but no one appeared; at two o'clock in the afternoon, he decided to go home.
 A. one
 B. two
 C. three
 D. none

____ 12. Why is the following a compound sentence? She compared the cruise vacation with being trapped in a washing machine, but he thought differently.
 A. It's not a compound sentence; it is a complex one.
 B. It is compound because it contains two dependent clauses.
 C. It is compound because the clauses are joined by the preposition *but*.
 D. It is compound because it contains two independent clauses joined by the coordinating conjunction *but*.

____ 13. How many clauses are in the following sentence? Color reveals a lot about the chemistry of produce: orange says beta-carotene, red indicates lycopene, and blue signifies anthocyanins.
 A. one
 B. two
 C. three
 D. four

____ 14. The verbal most related to the <u>dangling modifier</u> error is the ___.
 A. participle
 B. gerund
 C. infinitive
 D. conjunctive

____ 15.   Which is the only verbal that can be a noun, adjective or
adverb depending on its use in the sentence?
A.   participle
B.   gerund
C.   infinitive
D.   conjunctive

____ 16.   What type of clause is underlined in the following sentence?
Jerry polished the trophy <u>that he won for winning the
bowling league.</u>
A.   dependent
B.   independent
C.   subordinate
D.   Both A and C are correct.

____ 17.   Although the underlined section in question 16 contains a
preposition as well as noun, what is its part of speech in
that sentence?
A.   verb
B.   adverb
C.   adjective
D.   pronoun

____ 18.   What's the most accurate label for the underlined section
in the following sentence?
Bob Dylan, <u>one of the great American songwriters</u>, was the
subject of Todd Haynes' documentary.
A.   participial phrase
B.   sentence subject
C.   predicate nominative
D.   appositive phrase

____ 19.   Why is the following sentence a run-on?
You'll really like this new convertible of Volvo's, it's
wonderfully sporty yet truly safe.
A.   It begins with a dependent clause, which should come last.
B.   It should only be written as two separate sentences.
C.   It lacks an independent clause.
D.   Its two independent clauses are improperly joined;
they need to be connected either with a semicolon or
with a coordinating conjunction and a comma.

____ 20.   A verbal can never be a _____.
A.   subject
B.   adverb
C.   phrase
D.   clause

EXERCISE 24 • PUNCTUATION

Purpose   To bring clarity and proper meter to your writing with correct punctuation.

Reference   "When Words Collide" (9/e), Chapter 7

PART ONE

1–25 Directions

Complete the following sentences by selecting the correctly punctuated choice.

____ 1.   You can talk about this issue all day _____ but you won't change my mind.
A. long,
B. long;

____ 2.   The counterfeit by _____ had been hanging in the Museum of Modern Art is now in the possession of Spanish authorities.
A. Picasso that
B. Picasso, that

____ 3.   Alison is a _____ architect.
A. well known
B. well-known

____ 4.   E. Harrison Smythe is a _____ patron of the arts.
A. very-influential
B. very influential

____ 5.   Wow! This is a _____ exercise.
A. surprisingly easy
B. surprisingly-easy

____ 6.   A warm front is expected in the region early next _____ that should also bring rain and high winds.
A. week, however,
B. week; however,
C. week; however

____ 7. He asked _____
A. , Where's the television remote?
B. "where's the television remote"?
C. , "Where's the television remote?"
D. , "where's the television remote"?

____ 8. That speech was a _____ mess.
A. disorganized irrational
B. disorganized, irrational

____ 9. The protestors told the mayor _____
A. , "to stand for justice and not for business."
B. "to stand for justice and not for business."

____ 10. We really missed you during your _____ absence.
A. three week's
B. three weeks
C. three weeks'

____ 11. The quarterback _____ and rifled a touchdown pass to the speedy receiver.
A. dropped back
B. dropped back,

____ 12. This home will soon be _____
A. ours.
B. our's.
C. ours'.

____ 13. You've crossed my mind many times _____ why is it you never stay?
A. ,
B. ;

____ 14. The man _____ is acting strangely.
A. carrying the tattered briefcase
B. , carrying the tattered briefcase,

____ 15. Journalists are only human _____ readers can be harsh critics.
A. , nevertheless,
B. ; nevertheless
C. ; nevertheless,

____ 16. Labor and management _____ have had their share of disagreements.
A. not surprisingly
B. , not surprisingly,
C. — not surprisingly —

___ 17.   Have you read _____
           A.   "Sense and Sensibility?"
           B.   "Sense and Sensibility"?

___ 18.   _____ has damaged his health.
           A.   Working around toxic chemicals,
           B.   Working around toxic chemicals

___ 19.   _____ the challenger asked the incumbent.
           A.   "Where's the beef"?
           B.   "Where's the beef?"
           C.   "Where's the beef?",

___ 20.   He will return from vacation in three _____.
           A.   week's
           B.   weeks'
           C.   weeks

___ 21.   He paid $25,000 for the _____.
           A.   200-year old book
           B.   200 year-old book
           C.   200-year-old book

___ 22.   Judge Olson will order another investigation _____ she
       believes the primary evidence is tainted.
           A.   because
           B.   , because

___ 23.   Here's what management proposes to _____ shut down
       the production line, retool the machinery and reduce the
       shift periods.
           A.   do,
           B.   do;
           C.   do:

___ 24.   _____ of the county's farmland is under water.
           A.   Two thirds
           B.   Two-thirds

___ 25.   Tom bought two suits _____
           A.   (the three button kind.)
           B.   (the three-button kind).
           C.   (the three-button kind.)

PART TWO

26–35 Directions

Read the following sentences to determine whether they contain punctuation errors. If you think a sentence has an error, choose an answer that corrects it. If you think the sentence is correct, select C.

____ 26. He's a terrific snowboarder but an inept downhill skier.
A. Insert a comma after "snowboarder."
B. Change "He's" to "He is."
C. The sentence is correct.

____ 27. The torrential rains were unyielding; making driving a deadly nightmare.
A. Delete the semicolon.
B. Replace the semicolon with a comma.
C. The sentence is correct.

____ 28. Long thought to be relatively flat and shaped like Frisbees, some galaxies actually are oblong in shape, this has prompted some scientists to call for more studies.
A. A comma splice creates a run-on sentence; insert a semicolon after *shape.*
B. A comma is needed between the word *flat* and the conjunction *and.*
C. The sentence is correct.

____ 29. Did you see that article titled Greening My (City) Alley in "Mother Earth" magazine? I did; and believe me, it had a tremendous influence on me.
A. Replace the semicolon with a comma.
B. Enclose the article title in quotation marks.
C. The sentences are correct.

____ 30. Susan Butler says she's ready, "to stand on a stump and shout" if that's what it takes to get the city council's attention.
A. A comma is not needed before the partial quotation.
B. The quotation marks should be deleted.
C. The sentence is correct.

____ 31. She enjoys sailing, but prefers to avoid the boating resorts that so many well-heeled tourists enjoy.
A. No comma is needed between *sailing* and *but.*
B. A hyphen is not needed after *well.*
C. The sentence is correct.

____ 32.   I came to your well-publicized lecture to get the real story about the eco-terrorism trial, not to hear a litany of old war stories.
- A. Delete the comma between *trial* and *not.*
- B. Delete the hyphen between *well* and *publicized.*
- C. The sentence is correct.

____ 33.   "Fight all unfair taxes!" the candidate urged the audience in a strongly-worded attack.
- A. The exclamation point should be outside the quotation marks.
- B. A hyphen is not needed between *strongly* and *worded.*
- C. The sentence is correct.

____ 34.   I refuse to support Anderson, because I oppose his position on taxes.
- A. Delete the comma between *Anderson* and *because.*
- B. Replace the comma with a semicolon.
- C. The sentence is correct.

____ 35.   The defendant, fled the courtroom in the midst of his sentencing.
- A. Insert a comma after *courtroom.*
- B. Delete the comma after *defendant.*
- C. The sentence is correct.

NAME _____   SCORE _____

EXERCISE 25 • EDITING FOR GRAMMAR, PUNCTUATION, WORD USE AND SPELLING

Purpose   To incorporate "When Words Collide" readings and workbook exercises into a comprehensive editing exercise that tests a wide range of grammatical principles.

Reference   "When Words Collide" (9/e), all chapters and your dictionary

Directions   Review the following sentences and correct all errors in grammar, punctuation, word use and spelling. Look for ways to be more concise. Edit on this sheet. **Look carefully!**

1. Because I disagree with her in principal, I won't try and convince her that this project is pure folley.

2. The lightening which hit several of the trailer homes' was responsable also, for several deaths in Canton.

3. The pirate captain, entertained we sailors with his tales of adventure and lonliness.

4. In my judgement, everyone should complete his financial questionaire before proceding with this investment scheme.

5. The people that taut that math course need to be fired!

6. The victory that alluded the team for so long is finally in their grasp.

7. Tom is one of those workers that never seems to tire of a new challendge.

8. The company president has refused to meet with the media today, however a press conferrence will be called by the public relations department tomorrow.

9. Concerned that passage would lead to a rash of lawsuits, the loitering ordnance was defeated by the council, by a unanimous vote of 6-0.

10. The police claims that it's anti-drug efforts have had profound affects in the downtown neighborhood.

11. His plan is comprised of seven discreet stages.

12. The board is not anxious to take this new public safty plan any farther.

13. None of these cigarette brands are superior to low-tar M/Pha/Zema, in fact " Zema" is the most unique tobbaco product which I have ever encountered.

14. Due to child resistent caps on pill containers childrens' deaths from aspirin overdose has been reduced by over 80%.

15. Although we failed to acheive concensus on this issue, we certainly can site our collegiality as a marked improvment in our style of deliberation.

16. The City Counsel has postponed it's regular monthly meeting, due to a power failure which hit the City Hall complex this afternoon.

17. Mayor Helen Jennings was killed, instantly this morning, when the sport utility vehicle which she was driving collided with a telephone poll.

18. What the eyes see excite the brain.

19. Inflation is one of those economic evil's which tends to perpetuate itself.

20. I fail to understand you're rational for this decision; but it's a decision I will support.

EXERCISE 26 • THIS SENTENCE IS <u>CORRECT</u> BECAUSE...

Purpose   To assess understanding of grammatical concepts, especially agreement, case, parallelism and punctuation.

Reference   "When Words Collide" (9/e), Chapters 6 and 7

Directions All of the sentences in this exercise are correct. From the three choices offered, select the answer that best explains *why* the sentence is correct.

____ 1. How do you think this decision will affect the next election?
   A. The writer keeps this as a declarative sentence.
   B. The writer makes the correct *affect/effect* choice because a noun, not a verb, is needed.
   C. The writer makes the correct *affect/effect* choice because a verb, not a noun, is needed.

____ 2. The number of firefighters applying for early retirement has declined dramatically in the last three years.
   A. The objective case is used properly.
   B. The subject and the verb agree.
   C. The passive voice actually helps this sentence.

____ 3. Running marathons, creating metal sculptures and volunteering at the food bank keep George and Samira quite busy, thank you.
   A. Parallelism of the subjects creates a nice balance.
   B. The participial phrases are in harmony with subjects of the sentence.
   C. *George* and *Samira* are properly used as indirect objects.

____ 4. The professor reported that she enjoyed the students' papers, but she said that much more research needs to be done.
   A. This complex sentence is correctly punctuated.
   B. This compound-complex sentence is correctly punctuated.
   C. The writer keeps all verbs in the past tense.

____ 5. You're going to enjoy this new play; it's a Tony winner for sure!
  A. The sentence uses a parallel series of adjectives.
  B. The sentence avoids the passive voice, though this would have been as strong as an active construction.
  C. The writer properly uses two subject–verb contractions for economy and balance.

____ 6. Settling all his gambling debts, Uncle Joe crowed with relief.
  A. The writer skillfully avoids a dangling modifier.
  B. The passive voice works well in this construction.
  C. Linking verbs strengthen this sentence.

____ 7. Paris was the first city to address the issue of continuous city noise as a factor that negatively impacts livability.
  A. The writer avoids the erroneous use of *was*.
  B. The adjective *continuous* is properly used.
  C. The prepositional phrase is properly placed at the end of the sentence.

____ 8. We students are often hobbled by incredible debt upon graduation.
  A. This sentence avoids the use of appositives.
  B. The writer scrupulously avoids the use of the dash.
  C. The nominative case is used properly in the subject of the sentence.

____ 9. It's difficult to understand this year's budget without comparing it with last year's revenues and expenditures.
  A. The sentence successfully eliminates all internal punctuation except apostrophes.
  B. The writer stays in the same verb tense.
  C. The writer properly uses *compared with* instead of *compared to*.

____ 10. He is one of those writers who have never met a deadline.
  A. The writer is able to contain all this information in a simple sentence.
  B. By using the plural verb in the dependent clause, the writer keeps the pronoun and its antecedent in agreement.
  C. The strategic placement of the adverb *never* is the chief factor in this sentence's correctness.

Bonus Question

Examine the following sentence, and in the lines provided, give three potential errors that were avoided in order for it to be correctly written. (By the way, we see five possible pitfalls that were avoided.)

Searching for reliable clients has proved fruitful for the firm; however, there's always a risk in losing old customers.

_____

_____

_____

_____

_____

NAME _____   SCORE _____

EXERCISE 27 • THIS SENTENCE IS <u>INCORRECT</u> BECAUSE...

Purpose   To assess understanding of grammatical concepts,
                   especially agreement, case, parallelism and
                   punctuation.

Reference   "When Words Collide" (9/e), Chapters 6 and 7

Directions   All of the sentences in this exercise are incorrect.
                   From the choices offered, select the answer that best
                   explains *why* the sentence is incorrect.

____ 1.   Among the many reasons I like my classes are its
          unwavering commitment to excellence.
          A.   A change in number of the verb will fix the agreement
               error.
          B.   The sentence should use active rather than passive
               voice.
          C.   The sentence needs a comma after *commitment.*

____ 2.   Billy walked into the newsroom and immediately he starts
          shouting at the city editor.
          A.   The writer needs to use the same verb tense
               throughout the sentence.
          B.   The sentence needs to add additional commas.
          C.   The nominative case is used improperly for the subject
               of the dependent clause.

____ 3.   Everyone, including Sam and I, is going to the county fair.
          A.   The words *county* and *fair* should be capitalized.
          B.   The sentence contains a case error.
          C.   The indefinite pronoun should be written as two
               words.

____ 4.   Her daughter felt badly about their making a mess of the
          kitchen.
          A.   The *their* should be changed to *there.*
          B.   The linking verb should be followed by an adjective,
               not an adverb.
          C.   The preposition *of* should be replaced by *at.*

_____ 5.   Do you think that rising tuition costs will result in less
            students?
            A.   The writer needs to identify and fix the word usage
                 error.
            B.   The possessive form of *students* should be used.
            C.   The auxiliary verb should be *may*, not *will*.

_____ 6.   The board approved the nomination of the new directors,
            but the proposed slate of officers was rejected by them.
            A.   The improper use of the comma creates a run-on
                 sentence.
            B.   Changing from passive to active voice will create
                 proper parallelism.
            C.   Intransitive verbs should be used instead.

_____ 7.   A manager should always get to know his employees.
            A.   The word usage problem creates confusion.
            B.   The adverb *always* should be inserted before the verb.
            C.   The writer errs in using the possessive pronoun *his*.

_____ 8.   Neither of the writers, who currently meet only quarterly,
            want to join a weekly group.
            A.   By using the plural verb in the independent clause, the
                 writer creates a subject–verb agreement error.
            B.   The phrase needs to be restrictive, without the commas.
            C.   The *only* is misplaced and should be placed before the
                 verb.

_____ 9.   Her choice of dinner partners are alienating to her closest
            friends.
            A.   This sentence uses an improper antecedent.
            B.   The comma left out after *to* creates a run-on sentence.
            C.   The sentence contains an agreement error.

_____ 10.   The office said toxic stormwater is one of the city's biggest
            environmental problems which threatens residents' safety.
            A.   The writer needs a dash before *which* for dramatic
                 effect.
            B.   The objective case is used improperly.
            C.   The writer should change *which* to *that* to establish
                 restrictive meaning.

EXERCISE 28 • HOW MUCH DO I UNDERSTAND THESE GRAMMATICAL TERMS?

Purpose   To show understanding of grammatical concepts by properly identifying terms associated with them.

Reference   "When Words Collide" (9/e), all chapters

Directions   Select the correct answer from the choices offered.

___ 1.   A linking verb is never followed by a(n) _____.
  A. predicate nominative
  B. prepositional phrase
  C. predicate adjective
  D. direct object

___ 2.   The words *break* and *brake* are examples of what?
  A. acronyms
  B. homonyms
  C. dipthongs
  D. contractions

___ 3.   Which verbal is always a noun?
  A. gerund
  B. participle
  C. infinitive
  D. interjection

___ 4.   The words *completely destroyed* and *fatal suicide* are _____.
  A. nonrestrictive
  B. redundant
  C. indefinite
  D. relative

___ 5.   In the underlined portion of the following sentence, a(n) _____ is linked to a(n) _____ to create a(n) _____.

  Teresa is only looking for <u>long-term</u> employment.
  A. pronoun…noun…contraction
  B. adjective…noun…compound modifier
  C. adverb…adjective…dangling modifier
  D. participle…gerund…indirect object

___ 6.   Which part of speech modifies a verb?
A.   pronoun
B.   adverb
C.   adjective
D.   interjection

___ 7.   What is the underlined part of speech in the following sentence?
They yelled <u>boisterously</u> for more ice cream.
A.   pronoun
B.   adverb
C.   adjective
D.   interjection

___ 8.   What is the proper term for *children* in this sentence?
She was happy she had children who behaved so well.
A.   pronoun
B.   indirect object
C.   proper noun
D.   antecedent

___ 9.   What is the proper term for the underlined segment in the following sentence?
The doctors recommended <u>chemotherapy</u> to treat her tumors.
A.   indirect object
B.   predicate nominative
C.   direct object
D.   subject

___ 10.   What is the proper term for the underlined segment in the following sentence?
<u>Having visited the art museum</u>, the planetarium seemed like a good next stop on their tour.
A.   dangling modifier
B.   infinitive phrase
C.   dependent clause
D.   indirect object

___ 11.   What is the proper term for the following construction?
Choose a warm spot for planting winter veggies, they'll thrive better.
A.   compound–complex sentence
B.   oversubordinated sentence
C.   nonrestrictive construction
D.   run-on sentence

___ 12. What is the tense of the verb in the following sentence?
Andrea has written to the mayor five times in the past
month.
A.   present
B.   past perfect
C.   subjunctive
D.   present perfect

___ 13. A complex sentence contains _____.
A.   at least two independent clauses
B.   at least two semicolons
C.   one independent clause and one dependent clause
D.   only one clause

___ 14. What is the proper term for the underlined segment in the
following sentence?
I'll never use the subjunctive mood properly <u>because I
don't want to</u>.
A.   introductory clause
B.   participial phrase
C.   prepositional phrase
D.   dependent clause

___ 15. What is the case of the underlined pronoun in the
following sentence?
<u>She</u> never understood his devotion to such an illogical
belief.
A.   nominative
B.   objective
C.   possessive
D.   prepositional

___ 16. Some verbs, such as *sit* and *lie,* don't change into past tense
with conventional *–ed* endings. We call these verbs
_____.
A.   oversubordinated
B.   progressive
C.   irregular
D.   passive

___ 17. What is the proper term for the underlined segment in the
following sentence?
He put forth a hypothesis <u>that could not be supported
without evidence</u>.
A.   gerund phrase
B.   dependent clause
C.   independent clause
D.   prepositional phrase

____ 18. You can better understand the difference between *than* and *then* when you realize that *than* is often a(n) _____ and that *then* is almost always a(n) _____.
  A. conjunction…adverb
  B. adverb…conjunction
  C. noun…preposition
  D. adjective…adverb

____ 19. What is the proper term for the underlined clause in the following sentence?
  How do you feel about the letter to the editor, <u>which described police brutality,</u> being pulled from the website?
  A. restrictive
  B. nonrestrictive
  C. redundant
  D. correlative

____ 20. What kind of verb is contained in the following sentence?
  The panther moved swiftly through the grass to catch the running antelope.
  A. transitive
  B. intransitive
  C. linking
  D. auxiliary

EXERCISE 29 • GIVING POWER AND FOCUS TO VERBS

Purpose   To improve verbs that are weak and imprecise.

To choose the correct verb to match intended meaning.

To improve sentence clarity and conciseness.

Reference   "When Words Collide" (9/e), Chapter 9

1–10 Directions

Rewrite each of the following short (but weak) sentences with one strong, precise, and more meaningful verb. Be careful in your rewrite not to change the meaning conveyed in the original sentence.

Examples

Original Sentence: She imitated the actions of her brother.
Rewrite: She mimicked her brother.

Original Sentence: He shut off debate after 10 minutes.
Rewrite: He silenced debate after 10 minutes.

1. She was possessed of the courage to win.

   _____

2. He read lightly the notes for the test.

   _____

3. They complained constantly about the noise.

   _____

4. The potter hit hard and repeatedly the new clay.

   _____

5. She stared at him angrily.

   _____

6. He quietly but firmly expressed his anger.

_____

7. The doctor lessened the effect of the procedure by numbing the muscle.

_____

8. The council put a check on discussion for the new park.

_____

9. The employee made a point in support of more vacation days.

_____

10. He worked to get around driving through the new subdivision.

_____

11–20 Directions

These sentences suffer from the same malady: underpowered verbs. However, they are now surrounded by wordy constructions. Strengthen (and shorten) them by making the verb more straightforward and truly descriptive.

Example   The mayor treated her suggestion with disrespect.
Rewrite   The mayor _scoffed_ at her suggestion.
               (The verb _treated_ is weak because it is too general; we
               can do much better, especially because we know the
               mayor had a disrespectful tone.)

11. The loud rock music from the apartment next door really affected his nerves; it made him very nervous.

_____

_____

12. I approached you after class with a notification of my basketball competition dates.

_____

_____

w-118

13. He ate the spinach salad quite quickly, almost in a single devouring gulp.

_____

_____

14. The Smiths were very sorry about the destruction of their neighbor's lawnmower.

_____

_____

15. The sailor walked drunkenly down the alley, hitting one wall after the other.

_____

_____

16. These junk bonds have really caused damage to the company's pension fund in a devastating way.

_____

_____

17. The floodwaters ran over the banks in a violent surge.

_____

_____

18. The university president spoke in an extremely loud voice as he yelled, with an angry tone, at students who were protesting outside his office.

_____

_____

19. Bill's sports car slid over the icy road in a dangerous skid.

_____

_____

20. Sarah held back her thoughts about the staff reorganization, even though she was bursting to express her anger.

_____

_____

EXERCISE 30 • RHYTHM!

Purpose	To focus and combine ideas in sentences.
	To create order, prominence and subordination in sentences.
	To create rhythm by crafting sentences of varying length.
Reference	"When Words Collide" (9/e), Chapters 3 and 9
Directions	Write two sentences based on each group of facts. In your sentences, create the proper order and prominence of information. Sentence 1 should be complex; sentence 2 should be simple. The purpose of this alignment is to show the different pacing (rhythm) created by using different sentence types to present your information.
Example	A sudden blizzard hit the western part of Colorado last night. It stranded hundreds of motorists on highways and led to cancellation of all flights at the Denver Airport through 11 this morning. The snowstorm resulted in accumulation of 17 inches of snow and was a factor in several landslides.

Rewrite Sentence 1 (complex): A sudden blizzard that hit western Colorado last night dumped 17 inches of snow and was a factor in several landslides.

Rewrite Sentence 2 (simple): It caused cancellation of all flights at the Denver airport and stranded hundreds of motorists.

(**Note:** You don't need to use all the information given in your sentences. Just be sure that sentence 1 has one independent clause and at least one dependent clause and that sentence 2 has only one independent clause.)

1. A movie reviewer for the Claremount Times (his name is Geoff Hedges) proclaimed "A Witness Named Spot" the "worst" film he had seen in his life in his weekly column this morning. Several hours later, Hedges was found shot to death in an alley on Franklin Avenue, near his newspaper. Police say they are looking for a "person or persons of interest" in the slaying of Hedges.

Sentence 1 (complex): _____

_____

Sentence 2 (simple): _____

_____

2. Three people have died and 11 are injured in a fire in east Evanston. Fire officials think it is arson-related. It is the third fatal fire of the year. It occurred at the Woodbine Apartments this morning.

Sentence 1 (complex): _____

_____

Sentence 2 (simple): _____

_____

3. Striking aerospace workers have agreed to return to work tomorrow. They approved a new contract. The pact is for a three-year period. The vote was 450-17. The Seattle local has been in a work stoppage for the past three months.

Sentence 1 (complex): _____

_____

Sentence 2 (simple): _____

_____

4. Elvis Presley was special. He was, many would say, a musical titan. He had a troubled life, however. It was a life marked by drug use.

Sentence 1 (complex): _____

_____

Sentence 2 (simple): _____

_____

5. Nehru and Gandhi were two names that upset the quietude of the British in embattled India. Clearly, India was nearing a state of revolution, at a time when the British colonists spent a great deal of time attending garden parties.

Sentence 1 (complex): _____

_____

Sentence 2 (simple): _____

_____

6. An unlicensed Rhode Island social club was packed with people Sunday morning at 3. At that time, a fire destroyed the club. Screaming people trying to find relatives hampered efforts by firefighters to rescue people and to fight the fire. In the fire, 22 people were killed.

Sentence 1 (complex): _____

_____

Sentence 2 (simple): _____

_____

7. A heat wave is in its third week throughout the Midwest. It has produced record high temperatures, and as a result has claimed the lives of 13 people. According to a report by the Illinois Farm Bureau, thousands of acres of corn and soybean crops are in a state of ruin.

Sentence 1 (complex): _____

_____

Sentence 2 (simple): _____

_____

8. An overloaded passenger ferry capsized in a lake during a severe hailstorm. This happened in Finland today. A government spokesperson announced today that more than 200 people drowned in this incident. The spokesperson also said there were no survivors.

Sentence 1 (complex): _____

_____

Sentence 2 (simple): _____

_____

w-123

EXERCISE 31 • AWK!

Purpose   To detect, understand and correct awkward writing.

To identify common errors of writing and correct them.

Reference   "When Words Collide" (9/e), Chapters 8 and 9

Directions 1-5

Rewrite the sentences below to eliminate awkward constructions and to improve clarity and conciseness.

Example   There has this term been a very dramatic increase in the number of citations for disturbing the peace, according to the campus police who have reported this information. Rewrite into one sentence.

Rewrite   Campus police have reported a dramatic increase in citations for disturbing the peace this term.

1.   The Food and Drug Administration, an agency of the federal government, says it is planning to take steps to increase its oversight of a number of medical radiation procedures—the three most potent forms, exactly—which includes CT scans that are becoming increasingly popular.

_____

_____

_____

2.   The Senate Judiciary Committee will, for the next two weeks, hold hearings, which will be closed, on changes to election rules for primary elections.

_____

_____

_____

3. Heather Britt has a new novel, and it has been topping the best-seller charts for the last two months; and just yesterday, she has been named as recipient of the annual Platinum Pen Award.

    _____

    _____

    _____

4. The man, who is from Smithfield and is 28 years old, has two drunken driving citations already in the last two years, and now he has received his third such citation.

    _____

    _____

    _____

5. Calvin started his job, which was as a receptionist in the front office, but just two days after beginning work he suffered his first panic attack, which hadn't happened for the past three years.

    _____

    _____

    _____

Directions 6-10

Rewrite each sentence according to the instructions.

6. *Rewrite these three sentences into one, using an appositive.*
    Alan loves to play online poker. During his most recent game he lost almost $6,000. He was going to use that money to pay off his car.

    _____

    _____

    _____

7. *Rewrite this sentence to be more direct and grammatically correct.*
   Due to my cousin starting to rinse with mouthwash, his problems
   with halitosis have been reduced dramatically.

   _____

   _____

   _____

8. *Rewrite this sentence to fix the obvious errors and be grammatically
   correct.*
   Examining documents and records for two years, the university's
   football team who won the conference championship was found by
   the investigator to have recruited players who weren't academically
   eligible to play.

   _____

   _____

   _____

9. *Rewrite this sentence to be more direct and grammatically correct.*
   A British author with five novels to his name, the books by David
   Mitchell are incredible feats of imagination, elegantly weaving
   together several disparate storylines with a common theme.

   _____

   _____

   _____

10. *Rewrite this sentence to be more direct and grammatically correct.*
    An overlooked gem of a film, Starz Holdrom stars as an addict in
    Barbershop Blues, avoiding the glamorization or demonizing of
    drugs, but simply remembering them from the point of view of a
    survivor.

    _____

    _____

    _____

    _____

EXERCISE 32 • SPELLING 1

Purpose   To quickly recognize and correct misspelled words.

Reference   "When Words Collide" (9/e), Appendix A, your
                   dictionary

Directions   In each of the three-word sets below, underline or
                   circle the word that is misspelled. Secondary spellings
                   in dictionaries are incorrect. Correctly spell the
                   misspelled word on the line.

1. nauseous   wierd   excusable

_____

2. concensus   harass   embarrassed

_____

3. battalion   reccommend   canceled

_____

4. receive   percieve   germinate

_____

5. mournfull   pseudonym   resilient

_____

6. ellipsis   eliptical   harmonic

_____

7. sensatize   benefitted   profited

_____

8. discrete   discreet   caffiene

_____

9. rhythm   credability   colossal

_____

10. enviroment   occasional   immunity

_____

11. wholly   wholesome   goverment

_____

12. legitimate   reluctant   paralell

_____

13. corroborate   persistant   tobacco

_____

14. loathe   adolesense   apparent

_____

15. maintainence   missile   exaggerate

_____

16. questionnaire   withold   advertising

_____

17. dilemma   antecedant   aide

_____

18. preceed   innuendo   concurred

_____

19. wield   changable   yield

_____

20. supersede   proceed   indefensable

_____

21. criteria   criterion   accessable

_____

22. irritible   despondent   minimal

_____

23. pestilence   physique   definately

_____

24. epademic   misstate   innovative

_____

25. abhor   wintery   hygiene

_____

26. changeable   admirable   useable

_____

27. accommodate pronounciation digestible

_____

28. suggestable   accumulate   relevant

_____

Directions

In the passage below, identify the incorrectly spelled words by underlining them. Write the correct spelling directly above.

  Before I started acting, I never realized how accessable plays were as literature. I definately want to read more of them, even when I'm not preparing for a performance, partly so I don't seem oblivous in the theater community about the breadth and depth of plays out there.

  It's been a privalege to join the well-respected actors in this community, being axcepted by them. After three years, I'm no longer percieved as a newbie. I'm also excited that my love for acting is persistant —I don't see it abating anytime soon. I reccommend to anyone to persue your love for the arts, no matter your profession. Involvement in the arts can increase your emotional reach as a person, as well as expand the depth of your knowlege of the world.

EXERCISE 33 • SPELLING 2

Purpose   To further your mastery of spelling.

Reference   "When Words Collide" (9/e), Appendix A, your
                   dictionary

Directions   Review each sentence, and write the correctly spelled
                   word for each misspelling. If there are no errors in a
                   sentence, write *No Errors*. **Focus on spelling only;
                   there are no word use errors.**

1. I grew up thinking I had an inadaquate amount of protein in my
    diet, but it turned out to be untrue.

    _____

2. The exasperated sherrif had no idea how to procede with his
    investigation. He wasn't aware of any precedant for this kind of crime.

    _____

3. The city is being sued for its resistence to providing adequate
    accessability to its facilities.

    _____

4. She knew the day would come when her daughter no longer
    beleived in Santa Clause, but she couldn't help but fill at little
    desparation that her little girl was growing up faster than she
    preferred.

    _____

5. The trip leader was adamant that girls and boys would ride in
    seperate buses.

    _____

6. His curiousity about people was so vast; it made it easy to start
    talking about predjudice, and how to respond to it, at a very young
    age.

    _____

7. In all liklihood, our goverment's enforcment of our new enviromental policy will surly fail.

_____

8. Our school superintendant is responsable for this disasterous mess.

_____

9. Scott thinks it is wierd when his boss wields his power at the first sign of stress.

_____

10. She felt priviledged to work with such a conscientious and commited superviser.

_____

11. The counselor recomends more relevent therapy for supervisors suffering from stress.

_____

12. The best teachers enjoy children of all kinds and have a temprament to withstand, and then manage, a little chaos.

_____

13. The company promises a sizable investment in the city's power grid.

_____

14. I'm dumbfounded that you thought you could embarrass or harass me with this silly charade.

_____

15. Did you know that rubber shoes do nothing to protect you from lightening?

_____

EXERCISE 34 • SOCIAL MEDIA FOR GRAMMARIANS

Purpose	To identify and correct common errors of writing.
References	"When Words Collide" (9/e), Appendix A and your dictionary
Directions	Find the obvious errors in the following social media posts. Rewrite the posts to correct the errors.

1. Our no plan fundraising event turned out to be full of fun adventures. Thank you Braeburn family for sponsoring us! (6 photos)

   _____

   _____

2. Anyone have some free time to spare? If so, they should come down to support our shelter residents by serving up the amazing Thanksgiving dinner provided by our donors.

   _____

   _____

3. Hey theatre fans! Make sure and catch the amazing play "Smooth the Tide" by Stormy Kinton, adapted and directed by Jessica Stinton, running at the Brimblop Theatre until August 2!

   _____

   _____

4. This months charity what a wonderful group. Last year it was our biggest donation let's beat it this year!

   _____

   _____

5.   Musician Poppy Farver sports a cropped Bumbledom sweater and
     pairs, it perfectly with light, wash, ripped jeans.

_____

_____

6.   The NFL pre-season' kicks off this week! Try this tasty game ready
     recipe that only uses five ingredients and 10 minutes to prep.

_____

_____

7.   Say hello to wedding whiz and our favorite guy, Bernardo Truro —
     he's youre go to guy!

_____

_____

8.   Its National Donut Day! Its all about you eating fabulous fried
     dough, and so we hope you try and get to the nearest donut shop
     — soon!

_____

_____

EXERCISE 35 • A FINAL CHECKUP

Purpose   To help you evaluate your progress of grammatical principles. Test yourself, and review where needed. Your instructor has the answers.

Your performance on this checkup is an important benchmark for the work you need to do to establish core competency in grammar. Scoring 75 percent or better in each section is best. If you score below 50 percent in any one section, commit to further study of those concepts.

PART 1. KEEPING TO THE BASICS

These first 10 questions probe your understanding of basic grammar. Select the correct answer from the choices offered.

_____ 1.   What is *bunted* in the following sentence?
The hitter bunted the ball for a double up the left field line.
A. It is the only verb in the sentence.
B. It is the key word to making the sentence a complete one.
C. It is the "action" word in the sentence.
D. It is a verb in the past tense.
E. All of the above are correct.

_____ 2.   What is the subject of the sentence in question 1?
A. hitter
B. ball
C. field
D. line

_____ 3.   How many verbs are in the following sentence?
Kim knows to lock her car door, but she forgot last night and it was broken into.
A. none
B. one
C. two
D. three
E. four

_____ 4. What is the past tense of the verb *throw?*
   A. thrown
   B. has thrown
   C. had thrown
   D. threw
   E. through

_____ 5. What's the error in the following sentence?
   All of the dog owners and cat owners agree that it's in their
   best interest to let the dogs precede the cats in the city
   parade.
   A. The first verb does not agree with its subject in
       number.
   B. *precede* is misspelled.
   C. *owners* should be *owners'.*
   D. *it's* should be *its and their* should be *his or her.*
   E. The sentence is correct as written.

_____ 6. Which of the following underlined items is *not* an adjective?
   A. the <u>smartest</u> student
   B. a <u>really</u> bright student
   C. the <u>tallest</u> building on the block
   D. a <u>principled</u> decision
   E. a truly <u>charming</u> individual

_____ 7. What's the difference between a homonym and a
   homophone?
   A. There is no difference—they're synonymous.
   B. Both refer to words that have the same pronunciation,
       but homophones have different spellings and different
       meanings.
   C. Both refer to words that have the same meaning and
       the same spelling.
   D. Words that are homonyms may have several different
       pronunciations.
   E. *Homonym* is used instead of *homophone* in Great
       Britain and Australia.

_____ 8. What word correctly completes the following sentence?
   She is _____ about failing her first test.
   A. anxious
   B. eager

_____ 9. What verb below correctly completes this sentence?
If the number of students enrolled _____, more classes
will be added.
A. increases
B. increase
C. have increased
D. are increasing
E. None of the above is correct.

_____ 10. Which of the words below means "to cause to feel
resentment"?
A. peek
B. peak
C. pique
D. piek
E. None of the above matches that definition.

PART 2. FIX THOSE ERRORS

Carefully read each sentence in this section. If you think the sentence has an
error (or errors), select the best choice for correcting it (or them) from the
options offered. If you think the sentence is correct as written, select D.

_____ 11. Reporters should always try and protect their sources.
A. Change *try and* to *try to*.
B. Change *their* to *his or her*.
C. Insert a comma before and after *always*.
D. There are no errors.

_____ 12. The fire that struck the warehouse district last night
completely destroyed three buildings and injured six people.
A. Change *that* to *which*.
B. Eliminate the redundancy *(completely destroyed)*.
C. The corrections in both A and B are necessary.
D. There are no errors.

_____ 13. She is a well-known scholar who understands academic
committment.
A. Eliminate the hyphen from the compound modifier
(well-known).
B. Change *who* to *that*.
C. *Committment* should be spelled *commitment*.
D. There are no errors.

_____ 14. You're never going to believe who we saw today at the mall!
A. Change the exclamation point to a question mark.
B. Change *you're* to *your*.
C. Change *who* to *whom*.
D. There are no errors.

____ 15.   Each of her movie scripts have great box office potential.
        A. Change *have* to *has.*
        B. Change *scripts* to *scripts'.*
        C. Insert a comma after *scripts.*
        D. There are no errors.

____ 16.   Seriously, I don't think that the prosecution has proved its case.
        A. Change *proved* to *proven.*
        B. Change *its* to *their.*
        C. The corrections in both A and B are needed.
        D. There are no errors.

____ 17.   Billy said he was loath to describe how his experience as a community volunteer compared to his later work as a nonprofit executive.
        A. Change *loath* to *loathe.*
        B. Change passive voice to active.
        C. Change *compared to* to *compared with.*
        D. There are no errors.

____ 18.   The tennis player who broadcasters expected to clean up in the finals failed to win one point, losing decisively in the last round.
        A. Change *who* to *whom.*
        B. Add commas before *who* and after *finals.*
        C. Change *clean up* to *cleanup.*
        D. There are no errors.

____ 19.   The council approved the parking ordnance, but the auditorium bond proposal was defeated by it.
        A. Create parallel structure by making voice consistent.
        B. Change *ordnance* to *ordinance.*
        C. The corrections in both A and B are needed.
        D. There are no errors.

____ 20.   How has the defendant's behavior effected the defense's ability to persuade the jury?
        A. Change *defendant's* to *defendants.*
        B. Change *effected* to *affected.*
        C. The corrections in both A and B are needed.
        D. There are no errors.

PART 3. SPELLING COUNTS

Choose the correctly spelled word from each group of three words. Write the letter of your selection in the space provided. **If all spellings are incorrect, write an *I* in the space.** Alternate or secondary listings in a standard dictionary are *not* considered correct. Relax and give this a try!

_____ 21.   A. admissable   B. judgment   C. relavant

_____ 22.   A. gauge   B. embarassed   C. resistent

_____ 23.   A. fraudaulent   B. dillema   C. premier

_____ 24.   A. pasttime   B. pronounciation C. premiere

_____ 25.   A. accessible   B. weild   C. seperate

_____ 26.   A. accommodate   B. accummulate   C. reccommend

_____ 27.   A. tarriff   B. versus   C. superintendant

_____ 28.   A. procede   B. preceed   C. recede

_____ 29.   A. sophmore   B. supersede   C. definate

_____ 30.   A. seige   B. sieze   C. occurred

PART 4. PARTS OF SPEECH

Identify the part of speech of the <u>underlined</u> word from the options offered in the first five sentences. Then answer the questions posed in numbers 36–40.

____ 31.   She demands unwavering loyalty from <u>her</u> employees.
   A.   noun
   B.   pronoun
   C.   adjective
   D.   adverb

____ 32.   Tripping over the <u>fence</u>, he tore his pants.
   A.   adjective
   B.   gerund
   C.   noun
   D.   noun

____ 33.   The Panthers <u>traveled</u> all night to get to their next game.
   A.   linking verb
   B.   transitive verb
   C.   intransitive verb

____ 34.   Who wrote <u>this</u> incredible essay?
   A.   relative pronoun
   B.   limiting adjective
   C.   coordinating conjunction

____ 35.   This is the silliest exercise ever <u>foisted</u> on humanity.
   A.   linking verb
   B.   transitive verb
   C.   intransitive verb

____ 36.   How many <u>prepositions</u> are in the following sentence?
In an instant, she tossed my secret decoder ring to Tommy, who put it in his mouth and ran from the classroom before the teacher could catch him.
    A.   two
    B.   three
    C.   four
    D.   five
    E.   There are no prepositions in the sentence.

____ 37.   What kind of verb is *appears* in the following sentence?
She <u>appears</u> ready for the intense competition at the spelling bee.
    A.   transitive
    B.   linking
    C.   intransitive
    D.   conjunctive
    E.   None of the above is correct.

____ 38.   What part of speech is the word *you* in the following sentence?
Crying your heart out won't get <u>you</u> this job.
    A.   pronoun (as an infinitive)
    B.   pronoun (as a gerund)
    C.   pronoun (as a direct object)
    D.   pronoun (as an indirect object)

____ 39.   How does the word *this* function in the following sentence?
<u>This</u> is the best ice cream ever!
    A.   personal pronoun
    B.   relative pronoun
    C.   demonstrative pronoun
    D.   coordinating conjunction
    E.   subordinating conjunction

____ 40.   How does the word *this* function in the following sentence?
This salad should never have been served with so much dressing.
    A.   relative pronoun
    B.   demonstrative pronoun
    C.   possessive pronoun
    D.   limiting adjective
    E.   subordinating conjunction

PART 5. YUP, MORE SPELLING

Carefully examine each group of three words and identify the misspelled word, if any, in each group. If you think a word is misspelled, spell it correctly in the blank provided. If you think that all words in a group are correct, write *correct* in the blank.

_____	41. definate	adolescent	occasion
_____	42. aide	aid	tenets
_____	43. detect	legitimate	withold
_____	44. roommate	misspell	wield
_____	45. stationery	stationary	similar
_____	46. wiener	existance	vengeance
_____	47. leisure	noticeable	likeable
_____	48. reservoir	villain	villify
_____	49. hinderance	sizable	maneuver
_____	50. acquitted	cancelled	omitted

PART 6. WORD USE

See how well you understand the definitions and uses of the words that are often misused. Choose the word that best fits the intended meaning of each of the following sentences from the choices offered.

____ 51.   Nathaniel enjoys reading _____ novels.
      A.   historic
      B.   historical

____ 52.   Please _____ the book on the table.
      A.   lay
      B.   lie

____ 53.   Let's examine this issue _____ at our next meeting.
      A.   farther
      B.   further

____ 54.   She is an _____ to Senator Woodbridge.
      A.   aid
      B.   aide

____ 55.   Quit acting _____ you are the boss!
      A.   like
      B.   as if

____ 56.   Honestly, I'm not _____ to your point of view.
       A.   adverse
       B.   averse

____ 57.   Her plan is _____ of three distinct parts.
       A.   composed
       B.   comprised

____ 58.   I like bananas more _____ tangerines.
       A.   than
       B.   then

____ 59.   That professor has been _____ a manic composer.
       A.   compared to
       B.   compared with

____ 60.   This debate could use _____ critics and more diplomats.
       A.   fewer
       B.   less

PART 7. SENTENCE PARTS AND TYPES

Carefully examine the following sentences and select the correct answer to the questions posed about them.

____ 61.   What is the grammatical term for the underlined portion of the following sentence?
       He drove through the night <u>in blinding rain</u>.
       A.   direct object
       B.   prepositional phrase
       C.   predicate nominative
       D.   participial phrase
       E.   dependent clause

____ 62.   What is the grammatical term for the underlined portion of the following sentence?
       <u>Dreaming of a new life</u>, he sold his belongings and set out on a three-month trek.
       A.   independent clause
       B.   participial phrase
       C.   subordinate phrase
       D.   dependent clause
       E.   infinitive phrase

___ 63. Okay, let's get more detailed: What type of sentence is in question 62?
A. simple
B. compound
C. complex
D. compound–complex
E. fragment

___ 64. Here's another: What type of sentence is this?
Beneath the ominous calm has settled, since the recent uprising.
A. simple
B. compound
C. complex
D. compound–complex
E. fragment

___ 65. How many subjects are in the following sentence?
The French call the truffle La Grand Mystique because it is difficult to predict what conditions will help the fungus grow.
A. none   C. two   D. four
B. one   D. three

PART 8. A LONG DASH TO THE FINISH LINE

Think these questions over carefully and select your answers from the choices offered. Note the variety of grammatical areas covered in this large section that correspond with the ones you have dealt with throughout the exercise book.

___ 66. Which of the following lettered items is *not* a complete sentence?
A. Watch yourself on that slick sidewalk!
B. Stop!
C. That which you covet may one day be your millstone.
D. He contended his was the superior invention, which proved to be untrue.
E. Killing me softly, ever so softly.

___ 67. What is the error in the following sentence?
Houston's biggest enviromental problem is its sprawling highway system.
A. *Houston's* should be *Houstons'*.
B. *enviromental* is misspelled.
C. A comma should follow *problem*.
D. *Its* should be *it's*.
E. The sentence is correct as written.

____ 68.   Which word correctly fills the blank?
            Edith is a better swimmer than _____.
            A. he
            B. him

____ 69.   Which of the following underlined words is a noun and a
            gerund?
            A. The recently <u>completed</u> building is ready for
                inspection
            B. He knows that failure is completely out of the
                <u>question</u>.
            C. <u>Gambling</u> on his future could be costly.
            D. <u>Bumping</u> into the walls, he swore to buy a night light
                the very next day.

____ 70.   Which is the correct punctuation from the choices provided?
            The stock market continued its startling decline today
            _____ dropping 300 points.
            A. ,
            B. ;

____ 71.   The following sentence contains what type of verb?
            He reviewed his new administrative duties for the job.
            A. linking
            B. intransitive
            C. transitive

____ 72.   What's the error in the following sentence?
            Working through the night, the fire blazed stubbornly until
            6 a.m., when the firefighters were able to extinguish it.
            A. two misspellings
            B. sentence fragment
            C. wrong verb
            D. punctuation
            E. dangling modifier

____ 73.   Which of the following sentences is correctly punctuated?
            A. Firefighters repelled the flames on the ridge but a
                sudden windburst helped the blaze jump the fire lines.
            B. Firefighters repelled the flames on the ridge; but a
                sudden windburst helped the blaze jump the fire lines.
            C. Firefighters repelled the flames on the ridge…but a
                sudden windburst helped the blaze jump the fire lines.
            D. Firefighters repelled the flames on the ridge, but a
                sudden windburst helped the blaze jump the fire lines.

___ 74.   Which word correctly completes the sentence?
The hostess _____ the guests were eager to meet
left the party just before it began to attend to an ailing
relative.
A.   who
B.   whom

___ 75.   Your answer in question 74 serves as the _____.
A.   direct object of the transitive verb
B.   indirect object of the intransitive verb
C.   subject of the independent clause
D.   object of the prepositional phrase

___ 76.   None of your theories _____ sense.
A.   makes
B.   make

___ 77.   Question 76 deals with what grammatical topic?
A.   pronoun–antecedent agreement
B.   subject–verb agreement
C.   restrictive clauses
D.   nonrestrictive clauses

___ 78.   In the following sentence, how would you classify the verb?
Pixle is licking his fur.
A.   linking
B.   transitive
C.   intransitive

For the following items, select the word in the parentheses that correctly
completes the sentence.

___ 79.   This discussion is going (A. farther B. further) than I intended.

___ 80.   You should know that (A. its B. it's) never too late to start a
new career.

___ 81.   Neither the president nor his advisors (A. care B. cares)
who runs the meeting.

___ 82.   That was a (A. last-minute B. last minute C. last, minute)
request.

___ 83.   What sources have you (A. cited B. sited) to support your
thesis?

___ 84.   Among the 50 flats of delivered fruit (A. is B. are) only one
full of strawberries.

____ 85. The news media (A. is B. are) under attack again.

____ 86. The lab assistant (A. that B. who C. which) discovered a new protein is being honored at the next donor dinner.

____ 87. The county commission has decided to revise (A. its B. their) charter.

____ 88. (A. Her's B. Hers) is the best album of all.

____ 89. They extended the water main (A. farther B. further) yesterday, to houses outside the city limits.

____ 90. The number of original questions at voter meetings often (A. surprise B. surprises) politicians.

____ 91. Have you finished your project on "Stopping by Woods on a Snowy (A. Evening?" B. Evening"?)

____ 92. Phonetics is a field (A. that B. which) focuses on the sounds of human speech.

____ 93. He failed his (A. drivers B. driver's) exam because he didn't park correctly.

____ 94. (A. Who's B. Whose) jersey is sitting on top of the bleachers?

____ 95. (A. Three fourths B. Three-fourths C. Three forths D. Three-forths) of the shipment is missing.

____ 96. The story of his battle with addictions has been (A. well documented B. well-documented).

____ 97. The mayor called her opponent _____
A.   , "a feeble minded bureaucrat."
B.   "a feeble-minded bureaucrat."

____ 98. Her opponent responded _____
A.   , "That makes me twice as smart as you."
B.   "That makes me twice as smart as you."

____ 99. Climbing over the barbed wire fence, (A. his pants tore B. he tore his pants).

____ 100. You won't find a better grammarian than (A. she B. her).

EXERCISE 36 • ANOTHER FINAL CHECKUP

Purpose   To help you evaluate your progress of grammatical principles. Test yourself, and review where needed. Your instructor has the answers.

Your performance on this checkup is an important benchmark for the work you need to do to establish core competency in grammar. Scoring 75 percent or better in each section is best. If you score below 50 percent in any one section, commit to further study of those concepts.

NAME THAT ERROR!

1–10 Directions

Use the following code to identify the error in each of these sentences.
        A.   = Subject–verb or antecedent agreement
        B.   = Punctuation
        C.   = Case
        D.   = Dangling modifier
        E.   = Spelling

_____ 1.   Fresh and bursting with juicy flavor, bring cut watermelon for kids to eat on long, hot hikes.

_____ 2.   Running his car wheels over the curbs have left huge dings in his fenders.

_____ 3.   It was him who went to complain about the noise.

_____ 4.   Between you and I, this idea for a movie will rock the industry.

_____ 5.   Can you believe what Tom used as a slogan on his campaign stationary?

_____ 6.   The company will abandon their new venture because of the high cost.

_____ 7.   Sara wondered why her sister always managed to loose her dog during walks in Forest Park.

_____ 8.   Baseball is better watched as a live sport, I try to get to every game.

___ 9. I'm truly sorry, but Carlos and I cannot accomodate your request.

___ 10. Once he donned the pizza hat, studying with he became impossible.

AGREEMENT

11–20 Directions

Make the correct selection from the choices provided.

___ 11. The number of tape cassettes sold _____ decreased since CDs were released.
A. has
B. have

___ 12. He is one of those managers who _____ the hardest time making on-the-spot decisions.
A. has
B. have

___ 13. The rate of influenza cases _____ dropping, according to county health officials.
A. is
B. are

___ 14. Do you think I'm more trustworthy than _____?
A. he
B. him

___ 15. Five million board feet of plywood _____ been shipped to the war-torn country.
A. has
B. have

___ 16. The United Auto Workers says that _____ will set a strike deadline tonight.
A. it
B. they

___ 17. None of our muffins _____ dairy.
A. include
B. includes

___ 18. This is a tough assignment for _____ students.
    A. us
    B. we

___ 19. Two-thirds of the office building _____ under water.
    A. is
    B. are

___ 20. Building all those national monuments _____ given her a monumental ego.
    A. has
    B. have

CASE

21–25 Directions

Make the correct selection from the choices provided.

___ 21. The candidate _____ the newspaper endorsed was arrested last night on charges of embezzlement.
    A. who
    B. whom

___ 22. Corey and _____ are getting married next month.
    A. her
    B. she

___ 23. This is the candidate _____ the party faithful believe will be the next state treasurer.
    A. who
    B. whom

___ 24. Do you think that Sarah is smarter than _____?
    A. he
    B. him

___ 25. The university is deeply interested in _____ alumni.
    A. its
    B. their

ANTECEDENTS

26–30 Directions

Make the correct selection from the choices provided. Look carefully for the proper antecedent!

___ 26. Mary is the only one of the employees who _____ how to fix the copier.
  A. know
  B. knows

___ 27. Neither of the mothers has submitted _____ vote for next year's class representative.
  A. her
  B. their

___ 28. I understand why you chose those criteria; I just don't agree with _____.
  A. it
  B. them

___ 29. Sarah is one of those students who always _____ an extra pencil and eraser to share.
  A. has
  B. have

___ 30. I found Harold's report to be very interesting, but I'm afraid that the panel of judges was not impressed by _____.
  A. it
  B. him

IDENTIFICATION OF SENTENCE ELEMENTS

31–35 Directions

Identify the underlined sentence element by indicating the correct choice.

___ 31. Four hours of <u>sleep</u> is all new graduate students can expect to get.
  A. object of preposition
  B. subject
  C. direct object
  D. predicate nominative

____ 32.   <u>Flipping through the operations manual</u>, Carla searched desperately for instructions on how to reduce the green hue on her TV screen.
A. independent clause
B. adjectival clause
C. dependent clause
D. participial phrase

____ 33.   The reporter revealed <u>that the firm's money had been sunk into junk bonds</u>.
A. dependent clause
B. participial phrase
C. gerund phrase as subject
D. independent clause

____ 34.   The analyst said that stocks <u>are sinking</u> to new lows.
A. gerund
B. linking verb
C. transitive verb
D. intransitive verb

____ 35.   Albert, who almost didn't make it to the wedding, was <u>the best man</u>.
A. predicate nominative
B. predicate adjective
C. direct object
D. indirect object

SPELLING

36–50 Directions

Underline the misspelled word in each item. In the line provided, write its correct spelling. If all spellings are correct, write *Correct* on the line.

_____ 36. A. existance   B. environment   C. procedure

_____ 37. A. similar   B. commitment   C. superintendant

_____ 38. A. proceed   B. precede   C. recede

_____ 39. A. imminent   B. eminent   C. definate

_____ 40. A. hygeine   B. fierce   C. weird

_____ 41. A. resistant   B. tremendous   C. irresistible

_____ 42. A. accommodate   B. accumulate   C. dilemma

_____ 43. A. aid   B. forteen   C. aide

____ 65. _____ picking up the takeout tonight?
    A. Whos'
    B. Who's
    C. Who'se

WORD USE

66–80 Directions

Select the correct answer from the choices offered.

____ 66. The government authorized massive _____ to the war-torn country.
    A. aid
    B. aide

____ 67. Hendrickson admits that he _____ Internet dating.
    A. loaths
    B. loathes

____ 68. Don't you think we should seek legal _____ on this issue?
    A. council
    B. counsel

____ 69. Wilson is one of those politicians _____ you love to hate.
    A. that
    B. who
    C. whom

____ 70. The town council expressed outrage about his _____ activities.
    A. elicit
    B. illicit

____ 71. Columnists have compared his rambling speech _____ a blindfolded walk down a busy street.
    A. to
    B. with

____ 72. Are you _____ about this new opportunity?
    A. anxious
    B. eager

___ 73.   Yours is one of the most _____ presentations I
          have heard in a long time.
          A.   affective
          B.   effective

___ 74.   The project plan is _____ five distinct stages.
          A.   comprised of
          B.   composed of

___ 75.   The critics seem _____ excited about this new
          animation technique.
          A.   real
          B.   really

___ 76.   It looks _____ we're in for a harsh winter.
          A.   like
          B.   as if

___ 77.   His new marketing plan surely will be a _____
          success.
          A.   proven
          B.   proved

___ 78.   Have you noticed the man _____ has been
          loitering near the tobacco shop?
          A.   that
          B.   who

___ 79.   The volunteer group has raised _____ $2 million
          for the playground projects.
          A.   more than
          B.   over

___ 80.   I sense that she is _____ to go to the reunion.
          A.   reluctant
          B.   reticent

IDENTIFICATION AND CORRECTION OF GRAMMATICAL ERRORS

81–100 Directions

Read the following sentences and determine whether they contain
grammatical errors. If a sentence contains an error, select the lettered
item that suggests how to correct the error. Note that the suggested
answers use grammatical terms, so stay focused. If the sentence is
correct, select D, no error.

____ 81.   Please return this woebegone wombat to it's owner.
     A.   Correct spelling of *woebegone*.
     B.   Change *it's* to *its*.
     C.   Insert comma after *wombat*.
     D.   No error

____ 82.   I don't think that the prosecution has proved their case.
     A.   Change *proved* to *proven*.
     B.   Change *their* to *its*.
     C.   Both changes—A and B—are needed to correct this
         sentence
     D.   No error

____ 83.   Buckle up as soon as you get in the car, it's the best way to
     protect yourself.
     A.   *It's* should be *its*.
     B.   Correct the comma splice.
     C.   *Yourself* should be replaced with *yourselves*.
     D.   No error

____ 84.   Their's a harvest moon out tonight.
     A.   Replace the comma with a semicolon.
     B.   The entire sentence needs to be in quotation marks.
     C.   Change *their's* to *there's*.
     D.   No error

____ 85.   Theirs is a tender and incredible love story.
     A.   Insert comma after *tender*.
     B.   Change *theirs* to *their's*.
     C.   Correct spelling of *incredible*.
     D.   No error

____ 86.   The man who police say they arrested for the crime has an
     airtight alibi; however, police aren't willing to drop the charges.
     A.   *Who* should be replaced with *whom*.
     B.   Improper punctuation has created a comma splice.
     C.   *Aren't* is an improper contraction.
     D.   No error

____ 87.   Wow! Your advice for taking tests has really yielded
     dividends.
     A.   Change *advice* to *advise*.
     B.   Correct the antecedent agreement error.
     C.   Correct the subject–verb agreement error.
     D.   No error

____ 88. Struggling to make ends meet by working three jobs.
    A. Eliminate comma.
    B. Correct the sentence fragment.
    C. Correct subject–verb agreement error.
    D. No error

____ 89. To Meryl Streep Oscar is a deliciously familiar name.
    A. Insert hyphen after *deliciously.*
    B. Insert comma after *Streep.*
    C. Correct spelling of *familiar.*
    D. No error

____ 90. Us reporters filed more than 500 stories on the foreclosure crisis.
    A. Insert hyphen after *foreclosure.*
    B. Change *us* to *we.*
    C. Change the passive voice to active.
    D. No error

____ 91. The argument which I am going to pursue in my closing statement is going to be risky, indeed.
    A. Correct the one misspelling.
    B. Eliminate the unnecessary *indeed.*
    C. Replace *which* with *that.*
    D. No error

____ 92. How has the defendant's behavior effected the defense's ability to persuade the jury?
    A. Change *defendant's* to *defendants.*
    B. Change *effected* to *affected.*
    C. Both corrections—A and B—are needed.
    D. No error

____ 93. They're bound to make a mistake sooner or later, and there error will come back to haunt them.
    A. Replace *there* with *they're.*
    B. Delete the comma.
    C. Replace *there* with *their.*
    D. No error

____ 94. None of the stockholders is going to press for a proxy battle, but the board knows they can mount a well-organized buy back campaign.
    A. The compound modifier doesn't need a hyphen.
    B. Correct the error in subject–verb agreement.
    C. Change *they* to *it.*
    D. No error

___ 95.   Now really: Can you justify she going outside official channels to solve this contentious issue?

A.   The colon is not needed.

B.   Correct the one misspelling.

C.   Change *she* to *her.*

D.   No error

___ 96.   She is the only one of the writers who truly understand what sells in this self-help era.

A.   Correct the subject–verb agreement error.

B.   Change *who* to *that.*

C.   Insert comma after *who.*

D.   No error

___ 97.   Traveling unaccompanied through the Kenyan bush, he was ever on the alert for ivory poachers.

A.   Correct the spelling of *Traveling.*

B.   Eliminate the dangling modifier.

C.   Replace the comma with a semicolon.

D.   No error

___ 98.   I can't tell you how wholly dependent I've become on my dictionary; it's heavy, but it's definitely a lifesaver!

A.   Correct the one misspelling.

B.   Correct the two misspellings.

C.   Correct the three misspellings.

D.   No error

___ 99.   Managing the avalanche of financial crises has given her a well deserved reputation for mental toughness.

A.   Correct spelling of *avalanche.*

B.   Insert proper punctuation to make *well deserved* a compound modifier.

C.   Change *has* to *have.*

D.   No error

___ 100.   You're going to be a truly fabulous grammerian!

A.   Correct the one misspelling.

B.   Insert hyphen between *truly* and *fabulous.*

C.   Correct the two misspellings.

D.   No error